Family in America

Family in America

Advisory Editors: David J. Rothman
Professor of History,
Columbia University

Sheila M. Rothman

OUR CHANGING MORALITY

MORALITY

A SYMPOSIUM

EDITED BY
FREDA KIRCHWEY

*A*RNO *P*RESS & *T*HE *N*EW *Y*ORK *T*IMES

New York   1972

Reprint Edition 1972 by Arno Press Inc.

Reprinted from a copy in
The Wesleyan University Library

LC#   78-169389
ISBN 0-405-03866-6

Family in America
ISBN for complete set: 0-405-03840-2
See last pages of this volume for titles.

Manufactured in the United States of America

OUR CHANGING MORALITY

MORALITY

☆ A SYMPOSIUM ☆

EDITED BY
FREDA KIRCHWEY

19 30
ALBERT AND CHARLES BONI · NEW YORK

Printed in the United States of America

INTRODUCTION

BY FREDA KIRCHWEY

THE subject of sex has been treated in this generation with a strange, rather panic-stricken lack of balance. Obscenity hawks its old wares at one end of the road and dogmatic piety shouts warnings at the other—while between is chaos. And the chaos extends beyond ideas and talk, beyond novels and scenarios and Sunday feature stories, into the realm of actual conduct. Religion has indeed found substantial matter for its words of caution and disapproval: never in recent generations have human beings so floundered about outside the ropes of social and religious sanctions.

But while John Roach Straton and Billy Sunday point a pleasant way toward hell, while sensationalism finds in new manners of life subject for five-inch headlines, and while modern novelists make their modern characters stumble through pages of inner conflict to ends of darkness and desperation, a few people are at work quietly sorting out the elements of chaos and holding fragments of conduct up in the sun and air to find what they really are made of.

No one seeks to argue chaos away. Certainly Mr. Straton and Mr. Sunday are right: Men and women are ignoring old laws. In their relations with each other they are living according to tangled, conflicting codes. Remnants of early admonitions and relationships, the dictates of custom, the behavior of their friends, their own tastes and desires, elusive dreams of a loveliness not provided for by rules—all these are scrambling to fill the gap that was left when Right and Wrong finally followed the other absolute monarchs to an empty, nominal existence somewhere in exile. But the traditional, ministerial method with chaos was not Jehovah's method. He brought order and light into the world; but the way of our current moralists has been to clamp down the hatches even though "sin" bubbled beneath. A few courageous, matter-of-fact glances into the depths have been embodied in the articles in this volume. The men and women who have written them have approached the subject variousiy; the fragments they have brought up to examine do not necessarily fit together. But none of these writers is afraid to saunter up to the edge and see what moral disorder looks like.

Some of them find it thoroughly disagreeable. They believe that old laws were born of old desires and find their sanctions in the emotions of men. They seek for new and rational ways back to the sort of stability provided by the traditional relationships of men and women. Others find in contemporary manners merely the disorder incident to reconstruction; they find there tentative beginnings rather than ruinous endings. They see chaos as an interesting laboratory, filled with strange ferments and the pungent odors of new compounds. None of these writers offers dogmatic conclusions—and in this they differ delightfully from our most popular novelists and preachers. They present facts, they analyze and interpret; they suggest directions, they even prophesy. But they never announce or warn or reprove. When these chapters first appeared as articles in *The Nation* it became evident that this exercise of thought was itself commonly held to be a simple blasphemy. Letters from readers came in scores charging the articles with the sin of intelligence where only faith and conformity were tolerable. Dogma is so deep in the bone of even the more enlightened and adult members of our modern world that the most modest doubt regarding the success of monogamy or the virtue of chastity becomes in some way an insult to Moses or Saint Paul.

It is interesting to see how many of the authors of this group of articles find a connection between the changing standards of sex behavior and the increasing freedom of women. Are women forcing this change? Or does freedom itself make change inevitable? Possibly only the woman in the isolation of the home is able to sustain the double load of her own virtue and her husband's ideals. Out in the world, in contact and competition with men, she is forced to discriminate; questions are thrust upon her. The old rules fail to work; bewildering inconsistencies confront her. Things that were sure become unsure. And slowly, clumsily, she is trying to construct a way out to a new sort of certainty in life; she is seeking something to take the place of the burden of solemn ideals and reverential attitudes that rolled off her shoulders when she emerged. That some such process may be going on is hinted at in more than one of these articles. Certainly, of the factors involved in modern sex relations, women and economic conditions are the two that have suffered the most revolutionary change; and men's morals must largely shape themselves to the patterns laid down by these two masters of life.

Much has been said about sex—and everything remains to be said. Largely, new conclusions will be reached through new processes of living. People will act—and then a new code will grow up. But along the way guidance and interpretation are deeply needed, if only to take the place of the pious imprecations of those who fear life and hate the dangers and uncertainties of thought and emotion.

CONTENTS

Contents

Styles in Ethics
By Bertrand Russell

Hon. Bertrand Arthur William Russell

is a mathematician, writer, and lecturer on international affairs and problems of government. Born at Trellech, England, May 18th, 1872. F. R. S. 1908; Late Lecturer and Fellow Trinity College, Cambridge. Heir presumptive to 2nd Earl Russell. Author of "German Social Democracy," 1896; "Essay on the Foundation of Geometry," 1897; "Philosophy of Leibnitz," 1900; "Principles of Mathematics," 1903; with D. A. N. Whitehead, "Principia Mathematica," 1910; "Our Knowledge of the External World as a Field for Scientific Method in Philosophy," 1914; "Principles of Social Reconstruction," 1917; "Why Men Fight," 1917; "Mysticism and Logic," 1918; "Roads to Freedom," 1918; "Introduction to Mathematical Philosophy," 1919; "The Practice and Theory of Bolshevism," 1920; "The Analysis of the Mind," 1921; "The Problem of China," 1922; "The A. B. C. of Atoms," 1923; "Icarus, or the Future of Science," 1924.

OUR
CHANGING MORALITY

STYLES IN ETHICS

BY BERTRAND RUSSELL

In all ages and nations positive morality has
consisted almost wholly of prohibitions of various classes of actions, with the addition of a
small number of commands to perform certain
other actions. The Jews, for example, pro-
hibited murder and theft, adultery and incest,
the eating of pork and seething the kid in its
mother's milk. To us the last two precepts may
seem less important than the others, but religious
Jews have observed them far more scrupulously
than what seem to us fundamental principles of
morality. South Sea Islanders could imagine
nothing more utterly wicked than eating out of
a vessel reserved for the use of the chief. My
friend Dr. Brogan made a statistical investiga-

tion into the ethical valuations of undergraduates in certain American colleges. Most considered Sabbath-breaking more wicked than lying, and extra-conjugal sexual relations more wicked than murder. The Japanese consider disobedience to parents the most atrocious of crimes. I was once at a charming spot on the outskirts of Kioto with several Japanese socialists, men who were among the most advanced thinkers in the country. They told me that a certain well beside which we were standing was a favorite spot for suicides, which were very frequent. When I asked why so many occurred they replied that most were those of young people in love whose parents had forbidden them to marry. To my suggestion that perhaps it would be better if parents had less power they all returned an emphatic negative. To Dr. Brogan's undergraduates this power of Japanese parents to forbid love would seem monstrous, but the similar power of husbands or wives would seem a matter of course. Neither they nor the Japanese would examine the question rationally; both would decide unthinkingly on the basis of moral precepts learned in youth.

When we study in the works of anthropologists the moral precepts which men have considered binding in different times and places we find the most bewildering variety. It is quite obvious to any modern reader that most of these customs are absurd. The Aztecs held that it was a duty to sacrifice and eat enemies captured in war, since otherwise the light of the sun would go out. The Book of Leviticus enjoins that when a married man dies without children his brother shall marry the widow, and the first son born shall count as the dead man's son. The Romans, the Chinese, and many other nations secured a similar result by adoption. This custom originated in ancestor-worship; it was thought that the ghost would make himself a nuisance unless he had descendants (real or putative) to worship him. In India the remarriage of widows is traditionally considered something too horrible to contemplate. Many primitive races feel horror at the thought of marrying any one belonging to one's own totem, though there may be only the most distant blood-relationship. After studying these various customs it begins at last to occur to the reader that possibly the customs of his own age and nation are not eternal, divine ordinances, but are susceptible of change, and even, in some respects, of improvement. Books such as Westermarck's "History of Human Marriage" or Müller-Lyer's "Phasen der Liebe," which relate in a scientific spirit the marriage customs that have existed and the reasons which have led to their growth and decay, produce evidence which must convince any rational mind that our own customs are sure to change and that there is no reason to expect a change to be harmful. It thus becomes impossible to cling to the position of many who are earnest advocates of *political* reform and yet hold that reform in our moral precepts is not needed. Moral precepts, like everything else, can be improved, and the true reformer will be as open-minded in regard to them as in regard to other matters.

Müller-Lyer, from the point of view of family institutions, divides the history of civilization into three periods—the clan period, the family period, and the personal period. Of these the last is only now beginning; the other two are each divided into three stages—early, middle, and late. He shows that sexual and family ethics have at all times been dominated by economic considerations; hunting, pastoral, agricultural, and industrial tribes or nations have each their own special kinds of institutions. Economic causes determine whether a tribe will practice polygamy, polyandry, group marriage, or monogamy, and whether monogamy will be lifelong or dissoluble. Whatever the prevailing practice in a tribe it is thought to be the only one compatible with virtue, and all departures from it are regarded with moral horror. Owing to the force of custom it may take a long time for institutions to adapt themselves to economic circumstances; the process of adaptation may take centuries. Christian sexual ethics, according to this author, belong to the middle-family period; the personal period, now beginning, has not yet been embodied in the laws of most Christian countries, and even the late-family period, since it admits divorce under certain circumstances, involves an ethic to which the church is usually opposed.

Müller-Lyer suggests a general law to the effect that where the state is strong the family is weak and the position of women is good, whereas where the state is weak the family is strong and the position of women is bad. It is of course obvious that where the family is strong the position of women must be bad, and vice versa, but the connection of these with the strength or weakness of the state is less obvious, though probably in the main no less true. Traditional China and Japan afforded good instances. In both the state was much weaker than in modern Europe, the family much stronger, and the position of women much worse. It is true that in modern Japan the state is very strong, yet the family also is strong and the position of women is bad; but this is a transitional condition. The whole tendency in Japan is for the family to grow weaker and the position of women to grow better. This tendency encounters grave difficulties. I met in Japan only one woman who appeared to be what we should consider emancipated in the West—she was charming, beautiful, high-minded, and prepared to make any sacrifice for her principles. After the earthquake in Tokio the officer in charge of the forces concerned in keeping order in the district where she lived seized her and the man with whom she lived in a free union and her twelve-year-old nephew, whom he believed to be her son; he took them to the police station and there murdered them by slow strangulation, taking about ten minutes over each except the boy. In his account of the matter he stated that he had not had much difficulty with the boy, because he had succeeded in making friends with him on the way to the police station. The boy was an American citizen. At the funeral, the remains of all three were seized by armed reactionaries and destroyed, with the passive acquiescence of the police. The question whether the murderer deserved well of his country is now set in schools, half the children answering affirmatively. We have here a dramatic confrontation of middle-family ethics with personal ethics. The officer's views were those of feudalism, which is a middle-family system; his victims' views were those of the nascent personal period. The Japanese state, which belongs to the late-family period, disapproved of both.

The middle-family system involves cruelty and persecution. The indissolubility of mar-

riage results in appalling misery for the wives
of drunkards, sadists, and brutes of all kinds,
as well as great unhappiness for many men and
the unedifying spectacle of daily quarrels for
the unfortunate children of ill-assorted couples.
It involves also an immense amount of prostitution, with its inevitable consequence of wide-
spread venereal disease. It makes marriage, in
most cases, a matter of financial bargain between
parents, and virtually proscribes love. It considers sexual intercourse always justifiable
within marriage, even if no mutual affection exists. It is impossible to be too thankful that
this system is nearly extinct in the Western nations (except France). But it is foolish to pre-
tend that this ideal held by the Catholic church
and in some degree by most Protestant churches
is a lofty one. It is intolerant, gross, cruel, and
hostile to all the best potentialities of human nature. Nothing is gained by continuing to pay
lip-service to this musty Moloch.

The American attitude on marriage is curious. America, in the main, does not object to
easy divorce laws, and is tolerant of those who
avail themselves of them. But it holds that those

who live in countries where divorce is difficult
or impossible ought to submit to hardships from
which Americans are exempt, and deserve to be
held up to obloquy if they do not do so. An
interesting example of this attitude was afforded
by the treatment of Gorki when he visited the
United States.

There are two different lines of argument by
which it is possible to attack the general belief
that there are universal absolute rules of moral
conduct, and that any one who infringes them
is wicked. One line of argument emerges from
the anthropological facts which we have already
considered. Broadly speaking the views of the
average man on sexual ethics are those appropriate to the economic system existing in the
time of his great-grandfather. Morality has
varied as economic systems have varied, lagging
always about three generations behind. As soon
as people realize this they find it impossible to
suppose that the particular brand of marriage
customs prevailing in their own age and nation
represents eternal verities, whereas all earlier
and later marriage customs, and all those prevailing in other latitudes and longitudes, are

vicious and degraded. This shows that we ought to be prepared for changes in marriage customs, but does not tell us what changes we ought to desire.

The second line of argument is more positive and more important. Popular morality—including that of the churches, though not that of the great mystics—lays down rules of conduct rather than ends of life. The morality that ought to exist would lay down ends of life rather than rules of conduct. Christ says: "Thou shalt love thy neighbor as thyself"; this lays down one of the ends of life. The Decalogue says: "Remember that thou keep holy the Sabbath Day"; this lays down a rule of action. Christ's conduct to the woman taken in adultery showed the conflict between love and moral rules. All his priests, down to our own day, have gone directly contrary to his teachings on this point, and have shown themselves invariably willing to cast the first stone. The belief in the importance of rules of conduct is superstitious; what is important is to care for good ends. A good man is a man who cares for the happiness of his relations and friends, and, if possible, for that of mankind in general, or, again, a man who cares for art and science. Whether such a man obeys the moral rules laid down by the Jews thousands of years ago is quite unimportant. Moreover a man may obey all these rules and yet be extremely bad.

Let us take some illustrations. I have a friend, a high-minded man, who has taken part in arduous and dangerous enterprises of great public importance and is almost unbelievably kind in all his private relations. This man has a wife who is a dipsomaniac, who has become imbecile, and has to be kept in an institution. She cannot divorce him because she is imbecile; he cannot divorce her because she affords him no ground for divorce. He does not consider himself morally bound to her and is therefore, from a conventional point of view, a wicked man. On the other hand a man who is perpetually drunk, who kicks his wife when she is pregnant, and begets ten imbecile children, is not generally regarded as particularly wicked. A business man who is generous to all his employees but falls in love with his stenographer is wicked; another who bullies his employees but is faithful to his wife is virtuous. This attitude is rank superstition, and it is high time that it was got rid of.

Sexual morality, freed from superstition, is a simple matter. Fraud and deceit, assault, seduction of persons under age, are proper matters for the criminal law. Relations between adults who are free agents are a private matter, and should not be interfered with either by the law or by public opinion, because no outsider can know whether they are good or bad. When children are involved the state becomes interested to the extent of seeing that they are properly educated and cared for, and it ought to insure that the father does his duty by them in the way of maintenance. But neither the state nor public opinion ought to insist on the parents living together if they are incompatible; the spectacle of parents' quarrels is far worse for children than the separation of the parents could possibly be.

The ideal to be aimed at is not life-long monogamy enforced by legal or social penalties. The ideal to be aimed at is that all sexual intercourse should spring from the free impulse of both parties, based upon mutual inclination and nothing else. At present a woman who sells her-

self successively to different men is branded as
a prostitute, whereas a woman who sells herself
for life to one rich man whom she does not love
becomes a respected society leader. The one is
exactly as bad as the other. The individual
should not be condemned in either case; but the
institutions producing the individual's action
should be condemned equally in both cases. The
cramping of love by institutions is one of the
major evils of the world. Every person who al-
lows himself to think that an adulterer must be
wicked adds his stone to the prison in which the
source of poetry and beauty and life is incar-
cerated by "priests in black gowns."

Perhaps there is not, strictly speaking, any
such thing as "scientific" ethics. It is not the
province of science to decide on the ends of
life. Science can show that an ethic is unscientific, in the sense that it does not minister to
any desired end. Science also can show how to
bring the interest of the individual into harmony
with that of society. We make laws against
theft, in order that theft may become contrary
to self-interest. We might, on the same ground,
make laws to diminish the number of imbecile

children born into the world. There is no evidence that existing marriage laws, particularly where they are very strict, serve any social purpose; in this sense we may say that they are unscientific. But to proclaim the ends of life, and make men conscious of their value, is not the business of science; it is the business of the mystic, the artist, and the poet.

Modern Marriage and Ancient Laws
By Arthur Garfield Hays

Arthur Garfield Hays

is an attorney practicing in New York City. He was manager of the New York State La Follette campaign, 1924.

MODERN MARRIAGE AND ANCIENT LAWS

BY ARTHUR GARFIELD HAYS

"ARE we married?" This was a query recently put to a New York lawyer. The woman wanted to have been married, but wished not to be married any longer; at the same time she rather objected to a divorce. The man did not care much about it, so long as he could marry, or marry again, without too much inconvenience arising from the earlier entanglement. The lawyer's answer was so obvious that it might have been made by a layman: "How do I know?"

The two had been living together, had called each other husband and wife, and had in general passed as such, but at the beginning of the relationship each had felt that if one wanted to be free the other would not hold him or her; it was agreed that they should have no financial responsibility for each other and that there should be nothing about the arrangement which would make it last "till death do us part." In speaking of themselves as "husband and wife" they had intended the words to represent merely a formula of their own.

Now common-law marriage as recognized in New York State consists in a meeting of the minds—a contract. Thus, if two people live together as husband and wife this may be evidence of a common-law marriage. No formal agreement is necessary. But if there has not been even a private agreement of marriage their living together would be unimportant. If they wished to separate they would need no divorce, for they would never have been married. By passing as husband and wife they might gain the social advantages that come from a recognized relationship, and, since there had been no definite agreement, they might save the inconvenience of divorce if they wished to separate. Difficulty arises only when both parties do not agree that there was no agreement. Sometimes one party claims there was and the other that there was not. Then the very indefiniteness of the tie means added difficulty and publicity in breaking it.

In order to avoid future disagreement one couple made a contract in which they stated that they lived as husband and wife in order to avoid social stigma, but that as between themselves there was no agreement of marriage. The situation was trying because they always felt they were living a lie. Their answer was that society foolishly demanded either a penalty or a form and they preferred to provide the form. Fortunately, neither ever had to swear to the status and they felt that this contract—which provided for future maintenance of the wife and custody of the children—solved the problem or doubt of a life-long relationship. To those who made ethical objection, they answered that they were willing to contract on matters which concerned their wills, but knew it was contrary to human nature to contract on matters which concerned their emotions.

Not long ago in New York City a young woman who had scruples about promising to love a man forever expressed to the city clerk her unwillingness to use the form of marriage ceremony which he had produced committing her to love, honor, and cherish the man for the rest of his or her life. She said she was in good faith willing to contract to marry, and that she would do the best she could to make the marriage successful, but that was all; to which the clerk answered that if she were entering marriage in that spirit she should not be married at all. He was finally persuaded that the parties could be tied merely by agreement on her part to become the man's wife and on his part to become her husband.

If the law seems full of vagaries on the problem of entering marriage it is still more perplexing and technical when it concerns the question whether or not two people are still legally married when one has obtained a supposed divorce—so much so that it is not at all uncommon for a lawyer to be faced by a client asking whether or not he, or she, is really married. Some years ago a man was married in Philadelphia and later, having separated from his wife, went to New York. She obtained a decree of divorce in Pennsylvania, the papers having been served on him in New York. He married again and died a generation later, leaving a considerable fortune and three children by his second marriage. The first wife, or her attorneys, then discovered that the original divorce was not legal, since the Pennsylvania courts had not acquired a jurisdiction which would be recognized in New York. Since the man had left the estate to his "wife," there were complications. As the question involved the meaning of a will, the matter was one of intention and it was not difficult to prove that the deceased intended as his beneficiary the woman whom he regarded as his wife. But had he owned real estate at the time of his divorce the first wife might have had a dower interest, and had his status become one of public importance his enemies might successfully have charged him with bigamy.

Ordinarily, people are satisfied with a decree of divorce. It gives them the desired social status. Its technical legality becomes of importance only in connection with estates or the legitimacy of children. But a difficult question arises in case of remarriage. Legality depends upon the jurisdiction of the court. This can be acquired by personal service of papers upon the defendant within the State or a voluntary submission to the jurisdiction by appearing in the case personally or by attorney. But State courts claim and recognize their own jurisdiction even though papers are served outside the State. Under these latter circumstances, suppose a divorce granted a man in Utah is not recognized in New York. If he remarries in Utah he will have one wife there, while in New York another woman would be his wife and he would be obliged to support her there. If his wife in New York married again, she would be guilty of bigamy. In Utah it would be his duty to live with one woman. New York would attempt to make it his pleasure to live with another, and this on the ground of morality, for, although, ordinarily, the law of the place of the new marriage (in this case, Utah) would apply, yet this would result in his having two wives in New York. So on legal grounds we disregard the divorce, and on moral grounds we negative the second marriage.

Foreign divorces raise the question not only of jurisdiction but of recognition by treaty of a judgment of the particular foreign country. For instance, judgments of French courts are not absolutely binding upon the courts of this country, as are the judgments of sister-States. In the case of Russia, where any two parties by agreement or a single person by request may become divorced, there is no treaty whatever. Occasionally, cases arise where persons abroad have obtained a decree for a rabbinical divorce. Under the old Jewish custom a rabbi could pronounce a divorce and the law of the state permitted a decree to be entered upon his pronouncement. Some states and countries make bids for the divorce business; not long ago an advertisement appeared announcing that a divorce might be had in Yucatan for $25, not, of course, including the expense of travel. Questions of the effect of interlocutory and final judgments, of the provisions of a divorce decree forbidding remarriage within a certain period, of the *bona fides* of residence, of the jurisdiction of the court, of treaties with foreign countries may make it difficult to answer the question whether or not two people are legally married.

All this confusion represents a beating of wings against a cage—an endeavor to obtain a legal paper with a red seal which will avoid a situation which two people find intolerable. We are tending toward a new moral conception of the marriage relationship, well expressed by Premier Zahle of Denmark when submitting a new liberal divorce law: "It is based on the fundamental conception that it is morally indefensible to maintain a marriage relation by legal statute where all the real bonds between the parties are broken. This is a measure which certainly means a great step forward in the recognition of marriage as a moral relation."

Marriage is a status resulting from a civil contract, but very few people who enter into it know what this contract is. It assumes certain rights and obligations. What are they? That the wage-earner will provide. This is enforcible, at least theoretically. What else? That the parties live in an emotional and mental state designated by an agreement "to love, honor, and cherish," and, sometimes, "obey." This is obviously unenforcible. (I make this assertion despite the recent Texas case in which a husband obtained an injunction restraining his wife's employer from flirting with her.) The contract continues for life, subject to termination for causes which depend chiefly upon the place of residence, actual or acquired. If they live in South Carolina and stay there, the contract is indissoluble. In New York the contract may be terminated for adultery, unless the other party has likewise sought refuge outside of marriage; in Alabama, for habitual drunkenness; in Nevada, for neglect to provide for one year; in Kentucky and New Hampshire, for joining a religious sect which believes marriages unlawful; in New Jersey, for extreme cruelty; in Wisconsin, if the parties have voluntarily lived separately for five years; in Massachusetts and a host of other States, for desertion; in Pennsylvania and Oregon, for personal indignities or conduct rendering life burdensome; in Vermont, for intolerable severity; in France, if the parties have other emotional interests; in Denmark, by consent; in Russia, by request. Of course, in most of these states there are other grounds, but the result is that either party can bring about a situation which permits divorce or can make life so intolerable for the other that he or she consents to it. But these grounds must arise subsequent to marriage; the agreement cannot be made in advance.

In life the duration of marriage depends upon the desires or consent of individuals. In law it is perpetual, subject to termination not by agreement made at the outset, or by later consent, but by court decree. At the time of entering into marriage people usually know merely that somehow, somewhere, some time there is a way out if the situation becomes too strained. Technically, since the contract is for life, a divorce is granted for a breach. Thus there is an implied term, as there is in every contract, that relief is granted for a breach—but what constitutes a breach depends not upon the terms of the contract or the law of the place where the contract is made but upon the jurisdiction where relief is sought—a matter of which the parties ordinarily know nothing when they make the contract. Convention seems to demand that the parties know not what they do.

Modern society, this summary seems to show, has been moving toward freedom of contract in marriage. Those phases which concern the state, such as economic provision and children, must be conserved. But time was—and still is in some places—when marriage itself was a tribal or a state matter. Then it became a family matter, determined by the parents, and property and family rights and interests were the important considerations. But parents, knowing by experience that there can be no happiness without security—although there might be unhappiness with it—failed to take into sufficient account the emotional content, and, particularly in the Western World, there developed a certain freedom of contract in making a choice. To-day, when people have come to recognize the necessity of sexual and social compatibility, which cannot be determined in advance, there has come a demand for a further freedom of contract, to which society has responded by more liberal divorce laws. The laws which permit a divorce where parties have not lived together for a certain length of time make the duration of the marriage relation really a matter of consent. They mean in effect that a contract of marriage contains an implied term that it is to continue until the parties consent to its end, and in human relations this means until one party demands its end.

If a person proposed that the law recognize

a marriage contract which was to continue until either party desired its termination, he would be regarded as a wrecker of our institutions; but society is doing this very thing—obscurely, perhaps, as an after-effect, not as a preconceived design; blindly, and not with intelligent fore-thought. Many have suggested that marriages be made harder and divorces easier. But how revolutionary would seem a suggestion that marriage contracts be made in advance, conforming to the teachings of experience, providing for maintenance and custody of children and limited by the understanding of the parties; that those who, for religious or ethical reasons, wished to enter into a life contract be permitted to do so; that those who wished to enter into a contract to terminate by joint consent or at the option of either party likewise be permitted to do so? An objection that this would be dangerous assumes that people choose the present form only because compelled to do so. Individuals are breaking from the old conventions, and the law, usually a laggard by a generation, is following them. In forty-three States desertion is a ground for divorce; in twenty of them, desertion for one year. In seven States, failure or neglect to provide is a ground; in four of them, the period is one year. In some States, if the parties live apart for a certain length of time—in three of them for five years—that is ground for divorce. Is not this divorce by agreement? And by implication, since living together requires the willingness of two parties, the result is a contract which may be ended by either of the parties at any time he or she sees fit—after an intervening cooling period. Thus does freedom creep in by the back door.

Does this work harm to society? There is little difference in the marital or social conditions or in the welfare of children in Norway and Sweden, where there are liberal laws, and in England, where divorce is a long, complicated, and expensive process. No one could discover that he had crossed the State line from New York to Pennsylvania by observation of the state of society, the happiness or apparent duration of marriage, the welfare of children, or the social conventions of the people. Yet in Pennsylvania there was one divorce for every 10.2 marriages in 1922 and only one for every 22.6 in

New York. In South Carolina there are no divorces; in Oregon, the number of marriages to one divorce was 2.6; in Wyoming, 3.9; in California, 5.1. In the District of Columbia, the banner section, there were 35.8 marriages to one divorce. There, as in New York, the only ground is adultery. Yet San Francisco society seems as stable as that of Washington. Of course, the figures do not mean that seven times as many Washington couples as California couples, and four times as many New York couples, make a success of marriage or live together when it has ceased to be a success; but rather, that New Yorkers and Washingtonians solve their marital troubles elsewhere than at home. Thus, in Nevada in 1922 there were more divorces than marriages, because people married in other States repented in Nevada.

Whatever effect it may have on society, the extension of grounds for divorce which has taken place in the last decade, and the modern improvement in communication and travel, which opens other States or foreign countries to an increasing number, brings about a situation by which people, though not free to contract, do avail themselves of means which have the same effect. Revolutionary changes occur unnoticed, while our delusions persist and our sense of conservatism is gratified.

Changes in Sex Relations
By Elsie Clews Parsons

Elsie Clews Parsons

*is widely known as an anthropologist and writer.
She has contributed largely to scientific journals and
in 1922 edited the volume on American Indian Life
by various students of the subject. Graduated from
Barnard 1896; Ph.D. Columbia 1899. Fellow and
Lecturer in Sociology at Barnard; Lecturer in
Anthropology in New School for Social Research.
She is editor of the* Journal of American Folklore; *
Treasurer of American Ethnological Society; Presi-
dent of Folk Lore Society. Is author of "The
Family"; "The Old-Fashioned Woman"; "Fear
and Conventionality"; "Social Freedom," and "So-
cial Rule."*

CHANGES IN SEX RELATIONS

BY ELSIE CLEWS PARSONS

THE other day I listened to a conversation on marriage and divorce between a well-known feminist, her daughter, and an Episcopal clergyman. The celibate cleric and the younger woman were in fair accord: the institution of marriage was invaluable to society and had to be protected. Let there be no divorce, said the cleric, on any ground, at least within the church; children should be cared for by both parents, divorce being sought only as an ultimate recourse, said the girl, who was two years married and had a son.

The feminist was biding her time. Finally she said: "So much for the institution. What of the actual sex life? No divorce and continence or no divorce and intimacy with another?"

"The first, of course," said the cleric.

"Not at all; the second," said the girl. "And you, mother?"

"Oh, on the whole I'm for the brittle marriage as against the lax, the American way against the European. But most of all I am for tolerance in sex relations and for respecting privacy. Why not all kinds of relations for all kinds of persons? Just as there are now, but with respect or tolerance for the individual and without hypocrisy."

"Even if we did not agree," the cleric said later to the feminist, "we could talk about it as twenty years ago we could not. So much to the good."

"So much to the bad," said the girl's father, still later; "better for all of us the old reserve." The speaker was a lawyer with divorce cases in his practice.

Had we not here a mingling of currents from law, the church, feminism, and the younger generation which illustrates what divergency of attitude on sex and sex institutions or practices may exist to-day, even within the same cultural and local circle? Include circles of different education and locality and although the range of difference would be no larger the expressions of opinion would vary. Is the variation in opinion due to variation in experience or is it due to that contemporaneous lifting of the taboo on discussion which characterizes not only our talk about sex but about other interests as well? A remarkable and indisputable change of attitude, this release from verbal taboo, which often gives us a sense of change in general greater perhaps than the facts themselves warrant.

In the conversation I quoted the women were on the whole the radicals, the men on the whole the conservatives. This alignment was far from typical, I think, and yet in contemporaneous life, whether or not in opinion, women have been the exponents of cultural change in sex relations. The increase in the divorce rate, it seems probable, has been effected predominantly by women; about two-thirds of the total number of divorces are granted to women. (Of course the tradition that it is decent for the man to let the woman get the divorce must not be ignored in this connection.) This increase in divorce may indicate a changing attitude toward the criteria of marriage on the part of women. Women may be demanding more of marriage than in the day when they had little to expect but marriage. In other words, marriage standards mount as marriage has other relations to compete with. At any rate in the talk of women it seems to me that desire for integral satisfaction in marriage is more consciously or realistically expressed than ever before. Emotional and sexual appeasements are considered as well as social or economic advantage. What of the part played by women in changes in sex relations outside marriage?

Unfortunately, we have no dependable statistics of prostitution, but whatever decrease there has been in prostitution, and opinion is that with the passing of segregated districts there has been a decrease, may be, on the whole, put down to women, if only indirectly through an increase in illicit relations. Illicit relations are not subject to statistics, but that there has been an increase in them in this country in this century will be generally accepted, likewise that in this, too, the increase is due to women, alike more willing to participate in such relations and more tolerant of them in others. Again those curious suits for alienation of affection appear to be brought against women as much as against men; and theories of seduction by men have long since been sounding archaic to our ears. Even on the screen, the great present vehicle of traditional manners and morals, although rape is always in order, seduction is infrequent. Seduction with its complement of marital honor has been rendered an anachronism, through women.

The theory of seduction is affiliated with the proprietary theory of woman and, needless to say, this general theory has been undergoing considerable change for several decades. To-day women are not only not property, they are property holders, and property holding has become a significant factor in the social independence of women. Of this social independence, independence in mating is the most recent expression, more recent even than political independence, and less fully realized or accomplished. Indeed it would be rash to predict how this type of independence may be expected to come about; apart from the gesture, sometimes gay, sometimes merely comic, of keeping one's name in marriage, there is no conscious feministic movement, in this country at least, toward freedom in sex. The political emancipation of women came to us as a reflex from abroad, largely through England. Whatever the political effect of militancy in England, without the advertisement of the British suffragette American women would be voteless to-day. Quite likely the direction of emancipation in mating may be determined likewise from abroad, perhaps from innovating Scandinavia or from Soviet Russia, where the last legal word has been said on sex equality.

In the soviet laws on marriage and domestic relations there is no mention of suit for breach of promise or for alimony whereby woman proclaims herself a chattel, and according to the soviet code husband as well as wife is entitled to support if incapacitated for work. Incapacity for work is the sole condition which entitles either spouse to support. In other words, the Russian state has interested itself not in maintaining the proprietary theory of woman; but in providing for the care of man or woman in distress. Of such clear distinction American law is innocent. In American law the husband is still the provider and in this law lags but little behind current opinion, which holds that a married woman should work only when she has to. Dr. Herskowits tells me that this American attitude is so well represented in the Negro population of Harlem that in gathering statistics of employment as soon as he learns the occupation of the husband he can predict whether or not the wife is at work. Low-paid employment for the husband means wage-earning by the wife, and highly paid employment means that the woman is not a wage-earner. Surveys in other parts of the country have shown the same condition. These surveys have been made among wage-earners, and concerned primarily with the margin of subsistence; but familiar enough is the record in other economic classes of the persuasion that marriage exempts a woman from industry or professional activity. The standing controversies about married women as school-teachers are fully documented instances. The Harvard prize play acted last year on Broadway hinged on the rigidity of the alternative of a man marrying and sacrificing his career or pursuing his career and sacrificing his love. There was not the faintest suggestion that the woman might contribute to the family income and so render marriage and career economically compatible. The young couple, to be sure, belonged to smart Suburbia, economically a conservative circle; but there was

no indication in the play that the university intelligentsia did not hold to the theory of wifely
parasitism, nor that audiences might question the
theory. And I incline to think that few in those
Broadway audiences, although drawn as they
were from fairly composite circles, did question.
Wifely parasitism is holding its own.

In less invidious terms, where income permits,
the wife continues to be the consumer, the husband the producer. Conjugal partnership in
production, familiar in Europe, remains by and
large unfamiliar in this country. Outside of
marriage, on the other hand, the last years have
seen considerable lessening in our American
forms of segregating the sexes. Not only has
there been an increase of women in gainful occupations together with an increase of occupations
open to women, but between men and women in
business and in the professions relations are increasingly less restricted, influenced less by sex
taboo. There is more coöperation, more good-
will, more companionship.

Possibly this companionship between the sexes
at large will have a reflex upon marriage, and
marriage will become a more comprehensive

partnership. The question of the married woman in gainful occupations is related, however, to a larger economic issue. Our capitalistic and competitive economy not only suffers parasites and drones, it compels them by reason of its inelasticity in providing for part-time labor. The whole workday or no work at all is the notice given to women who would be part-day home-keepers, either in their child-bearing years or because of other family exigency, as well as to men who are aging or invalid. For this economic waste and loss to personal happiness and welfare there seems to be no promise of relief in prospect. Just the opposite, in fact, for women, since, given the increasing mechanization of housekeeping and the ramifying organization of hospital, nursery, and school, women at home may have a larger and larger part of the day on their hands and their functions become less and less significant. In this connection birth control has been for some time an important factor. As knowledge of contraception becomes surer and more widespread and births more spaced, even during her child-bearing period the home-staying woman will have less and less call on her vitality and energy.

Discussion of contraception has been active in the last decade or so; but curiously enough its significance aside from contributing to directly saner ways of life * has been little realized. Birth control makes possible such clear-cut distinctions between mating and parenthood that it might be expected to produce radical changes in theories of sex attitude or relationship, forcing the discard of many an argument for personal suppression for the good of children or the honor of the family, and forcing redefinition of concepts of honor and sincerity between the sexes. In such redefinition reciprocity in passion, emotional integrity, and mutual enhancement of life might share in the approval once confined to constancy, fidelity, and duty, virtues that are obviously suggested by the hit or miss system of mating and reproducing our social organization has favored. With little or no self-knowledge

* Dr. Ogburn informs me that his recent and still unpublished analysis of the census of 1920 shows that in localities where birth control is presumedly practiced the marriage rate mounts. He states also that in the country at large there has been a higher marriage rate in the last census decade and that the age at marriage is earlier.

or knowledge of men, a girl often marries in order to find out how much she cares or whether or
not she qualifies, and then when her experience
has but begun she finds herself an expectant
mother, and maternity begins to supersede other
interests. She may become a parent without the
assurance of being well-mated, if not, more tragi-
cally, with the certainty of being mismated. Advocates of the monogamous family would do well
to consider how essential to an enduring union,
at least in our society, experience in love may be,
together with restraint from child-bearing before
experience is achieved.

That neither such considerations nor other
changes in the theory of sex morality have yet
come to the fore in current discussion is perhaps
because the technique of contraception is still in
the experimental stage, perhaps because in popular consciousness the morality of contraception in
itself is not fully established. How is it going to
be established? I doubt if through rationalism
or rationalistic propaganda. Social changes, we
begin to know, are rarely due to deliberation, in
any society. In our society they are due mainly
to economic causes. Housing congestion in New

York will in time affect birth-control legislation in Albany; and fear of an overpopulated world will drive church as well as state into a new attitude toward multiplying to the glory of God.

As in birth control so in other matters of sex intimacy the growth of cities and the complexity of our economy may be the more potent factors of change. In very large communities there is an ignorance of the personal relations of others, an inevitable ignoring which contributes unconsciously to tolerance toward experiment and variation in sex relations. Indifference to the private life of others is almost an exigency of our economic organization. Attention is directed to the efficiency of the personality encountered and away from the individual means taken to induce that efficiency. What difference does it make to an employer how clerk or stenographer lives after hours provided he or she is competent, alert, and responsive to the business need? In office or in factory one may be but a cog in the machine and yet left larger personal freedom than in a more independent job in a small place or than in a household. Out of such urban influences—negatively, of indifference, and positively, of attention to personality *per se*—come opportunities for personal freedom that will set men and women to ordering their sex life to please themselves rather than to please society. That is, ordinary men and women; certain outstanding figures will have to continue to forego freedom. The President of the United States, presidents of banks or colleges, cinematograph stars, "society ladies," now and again a clergyman or a prize-fighter—all these will continue to be observed closely in their private life, and, like the gods and goddesses of other cultures or times, will have to conform to popular preconceptions of marriage or celibacy, chastity or libertinism. For them, as for other personages in folk-lore, individual adjustment or variation would be out of the picture.

Toward Monogamy
By Charlotte Perkins Gilman

Charlotte Perkins Gilman

*feminist, philosopher, writer was born at Hartford,
Conn., July 3rd, 1860. Editor of the* Forerunner
*1909-1916; Author of "Women and Economics,"
1898; "In This, Our World," 1898; "The Yellow
Wall-Paper," 1899; Concerning Children," 1900;
"The Home, Its Work and Influence," 1903;
"Human Work," 1904; "What Diantha Did,"
1910; "The Man-Made World," 1910; "The
Crux," 1911; "Moving the Mountain," 1911;
"His Religion and Hers," 1923.*

TOWARD MONOGAMY

BY CHARLOTTE PERKINS GILMAN

PHYSIOLOGISTS tell us that in all our long ages of animal evolution we have not yet completed the physical changes incident to assuming an erect posture. Psychologists may as plainly see that in the short centuries of social evolution we have naturally failed to complete the changes incident to our growth from tribal to national and international relationships.

Since we remained savages for some 90 per cent of the period of human life on earth, it is to be expected that the long-practiced tribal morals should have modified our characters more deeply than those evolved in the recent, varied, and fluctuating relationship of larger range. Yet we see, during the short period of progressive civilization, such swift and amazing development in some lines, such achievement in knowledge, in wealth, in ability, in breadth of thought, and nobility of feeling that our coincident stupidity and senseless misbehavior call for explanation.

The main reason for this peculiar delay and irregularity in social evolution is that it has been limited to half the race, the other half being restricted to domestic industry and to the still lower level of misused sex. Our specialized knowledge, power, and skill are developed through the organic relationships of the social group; as are also those characteristics of mutual loyalty and love, of truth, honor, and courage which are as natural to a human society as the distinctive virtues of ants or beavers to their groups.

Humanity's major error, the exploitation of the female by the male, has not only kept her at the lowest step in social progress—solitary hand-labor in and for the family—but has resulted in excessive sex-development through prolonged misuse. This has made her ultra-feminine, to a degree often injurious to motherhood; and him ultra-masculine, his social advance confused, impeded, and repeatedly destroyed by his excessive emotions. In social morals he has of course outdistanced her, as he alone has entered into the relationships which develop them; but he has carefully exempted his essentially male activities from this elevating influence, maintaining that "all's fair in love and war." Of her, domestic morality demanded but one virtue, sex-loyalty; her mate or master taking it upon himself to be both judge and executioner in case of failure. She might be a liar and a coward, lazy, selfish, extravagant, or cruel, but if chaste these traits were overlooked. If unchaste, no array of other virtues was enough to save her. In her household labors she developed minor virtues natural to the position; a tireless industry, an instinct for cleanliness and order, with great capacity for self-denial and petty economy. Speaking broadly, of a race where the young, though necessarily inheriting from both parents, yet are divided almost from birth in training and experience, it may be said that the social virtues have belonged to men, the domestic virtues to women.

Our present age, counting the incredible advance of the last century and the swift fruition of these immediate years, shows among its newly distinguishing social movements one of supreme importance. Within a hundred years women, in most civilized countries, have moved from domestic into social relationship. Such a sudden and enormous change, while inherently for the improvement of society, is naturally accompanied by much local and immediate dislocation in previously accepted conditions. Many are alarmed at what is considered "the danger to the home" resultant from the refusal of an increasing number of women to spend their lives as house-servants; they fear "the menace to the family" due to similarly increasing numbers of women who refuse compulsory motherhood; they are shocked at a looseness, even grossness, of behavior between the sexes which seems to threaten marriage itself. Few seem able to look beyond the present inconveniences to a specialized efficiency in household management which will raise the standard of public health and private comfort, with large reduction in the cost of living; to such general improvement in child-culture as will lift the average of citizenship and lower the death-rate appreciably; and to a rational and permanent basis for our monogamous marriage.

To understand rightly this trying period, to be patient with its unavoidable reactions and excesses, to know what tendencies to approve and promote and what to condemn and oppose, requires some practical knowledge of biology and sociology. Men, though as yet beyond women in social morality, are unreliable judges in this time of change because their ox is gored—they are the ones who are losing a cherished possession. The overdeveloped sex instinct of men, requiring more than women were willing to give, has previously backed its demands by an imposing array of civil and religious laws requiring feminine submission, has not scrupled to use force or falsehood, and held final power through the economic dependence of women. It is easy to see that if women had been equally willing no such tremendous machinery of compulsion need have been evolved.

But now that the woman no longer admits that "he shall rule over her," and is able to modify the laws; now that she has become braver, and above all is attaining financial freedom, her previous master has no hold upon her beyond natural attraction and—persuasion. Toward this end he manifests an instant and vigorous activity. Whereas in the past women were taught that they had no such "imperative instincts" as men, and the wooer, even the husband, sought to preserve this impression, now it is quite otherwise. All that elaborate theory of feminine chastity, that worship of virginity, goes by the board, and women are given a reversed theory—that they are just the same as men, if not more so; our "double standard" is undoubled and ironed flat—to the level of masculine desire.

Clothed in the solemn, newly invented terms of psychoanalysis, a theory of sex is urged upon us which bases all our activities upon this one function. It is exalted as not only an imperative instinct, but as *the* imperative instinct, no others being recognized save the demands of the stomach. Surely never was a more physical theory disguised in the technical verbiage of "psychology." We should not too harshly blame the ingenious mind of man for thinking up a new theory to retain what the old ones no longer assured him; nor too severely criticize the subject class, so newly freed, for committing the same excesses, the same eager imitations of the previous master, which history shows in any recently enfranchised people. Just as women have imitated the drug-habits of men, without the faintest excuse or reason, merely to show that they can, so are they imitating men's sex habits, in large measure. Those who go too far in such excesses will presumably die without issue, doing no permanent harm to the stock. This wild excitement over sex, as if it were a new discovery peculiar to our time, will be allayed by further knowledge. Even a little study of the common facts of nature has a cooling and heartening influence.

The essential facts are these: That all living forms show the tendency to maintain and to reproduce themselves; that some, in differing degree, show tendencies to vary and to improve; that after an immense period of reproduction without it (showing that as the "life force" it was quite unnecessary) the distinction of sex appeared as a means to freer variation and improvement; that the male characteristics of intense desire for the female, personal display, and intermasculine combat, as well as the female's instinct of selection, are visible contributions to the major purpose of improvement; that in the higher and later life-forms further and more rapid improvement has been made through the development in the female of new organs and functions for the benefit of the young; through her alone have come the upward steps of viviparous birth, the marsupial pouch, and that crowning advantage, the mammary glands; the female solely is responsible for the development of nature's aristocracy, Order Mammalia.

In the human species she adds to her previous contributions to racial progress the invention of our primitive industries, which were evolved by her in service to the young, and later carried out by men into the trades and crafts which support human life. In the developing care and nurture of her children she laid the foundation for those social functions of government, education, and coöperative industry which are so vitally important to social progress that we have called the family "the unit of the state."

This is an error. The family is the prototype of the state, a tiny primitive state in itself, often quite inimical to the interests of the larger state which has developed through the wider interaction of individuals. The state does not elect

families, tax families, punish families, nor thrive
where physical inheritance is made the basis of
authority. Where the family persists too power-
fully, as in China, there is a commensurate lack
in the vitality and efficiency of the state. By
restricting women to the family relationship,
with its compulsory woman service and domestic
morality, we have checked and perverted social
growth by keeping out of it the most effective
factor in that growth, the mother.

The world having been for so long dominated
by the individualistic and combative male, with
that vast increment of masculine thought and
emotion embodied in our literature, our religion,
our art, modifying all our ideals, it is not to be
wondered at that the newly freed women are
as yet unable to see their opportunity, their
power, and their long-prevented sex duty—race
improvement.

The collapse of the arbitrary and unjust domestic morality of the past will presently be followed by recognition of the social morality of
the future. Rightly discarding artificial standards of virtue based on the pleasure of men, we
shall establish new ones based on natural law.

Repudiating their duty to an owner and master, women have yet to accept and fulfill their duty to society, to the human race. This is not generally clear to them. In their legitimate rebellion against domestic service and compulsory sex-service they almost inevitably confuse these things with marriage, with which indeed they have been long synonymous. Some of our most valuable women, as well as many of negligible importance, speak of marriage as if it were an invention of Queen Victoria. Surely no excessive education is needed to learn that monogamy, among many of the higher carnivora and birds, is as natural a form of sex union as the polygamy of the grass eaters or the promiscuity among insects, reptiles, and fish. Monogamy appears when it is to the advantage of the young to have the continued care of both parents. This means that the parents share in the activities of supporting the family; it does not mean that the female becomes the servant of the male. Because of the united activities and mutual services of the pair love is developed, and stays. Such profound affection is found in some of these natural "marriages" that if one of a pair is killed the other will not mate again. Mated leopards or ostriches do not remain together because they are "Victorian" or "puritanical," but because they like to. They could form as many and as variegated "free unions" as Greenwich Villagers if they choose; there is nothing to stop them.

But natural monogamy is as free from sex service as from domestic service. The pairing species adhere to their mating season as do the polygamous ones, or even the promiscuous. Man is the only animal using this function out of season and apart from its essential purpose. These natural monogamists are not "ascetics." They are not dominated by religious doctrine or civil law. They fulfill their natural desires with the utmost freedom, but these desires do not move them out of season.

The human species, with all its immense advantages, has made many conspicuous missteps. Its eating habits are such as to have induced a wide assortment of wholly unnecessary diseases; its drinking habits are glaringly injurious; and its excessive indulgence in sex-waste has imperiled the life of the race.

Domestic morality vaguely recognized some

duty to society and sought through religion to limit masculine desires or at least to restrict their indulgence to marriage. But the desires of a vigorous polygamist are not easily restricted to one wife; and our polygamous period was far longer than that of the recently established monogamy. It is a most reassuring fact in social evolution that monogamy, naturally belonging to our species, has persisted among the common people and in popular ideals: even in "The Arabian Nights" the love story is always about one man and one woman, never of the mad passion for a harem! So with the accelerated progress of recent centuries monogamous union becomes accepted, and is carefully buttressed by the law, while religion, with commandments and ceremonies, does its best to establish "the sanctity of marriage." But as religion, law, and family authority were all in the hands of men, they naturally interpreted that sanctity to suit themselves, ignored the religious restrictions, and so handled the law as to apply its penalties to but one party in a dual offense.

Social morality requires the promotion of such lines of conduct as are beneficial to the maintenance and improvement of society. It will demand of both man and woman the full development of personal health and vigor, careful selection of the best mate by both, with recognition on her side of special responsibility as the natural arbiter. It will encourage such sex relations as are proved advantageous both to individual happiness and to the race. We are as yet so hagridden by domestic morality, with its arbitrary restrictions, and by the threats and punishments of law and religion, that we shrink from the broader biological judgment as if it involved blame, punishment, compulsory reform. Not at all. Men and women are no more to blame for being oversexed than a prize hog for being overfat. The portly pig is not sick or wicked, he is merely overdeveloped in adipose tissue. Our condition does not call for condemnation, nor can we expect any sudden and violent change in our behavior resting on foolish ideals of celibacy, of self-denial, or of "sublimated sex." It will take several generations of progressive selection, with widely different cultural influences, to reëstablish a normal sex development in *genus homo*, with its consequences in happier marriage, better children, and wide improvement in the public health.

It is to this end, with all its widening range of racial progress, that social morality tends.

Women—Free for What?
By Edwin Muir

Edwin Muir,

poet and essayist, has been assistant editor of the
New Age (*London*) *as well as dramatic critic for
the* Scotsman *and the* Athenæum. *He was a frequent contributor to* The Freeman.

WOMEN—FREE FOR WHAT?

BY EDWIN MUIR

IN the beginning of the Scottish Shorter Catechism there is a beautiful affirmation. "The chief end of man," it says, "is to glorify God and enjoy Him forever."

To any one nourished on the literature and thought of the last half-century that sentence, which defines the chief purpose of life as praise and enjoyment, comes like an audacious blasphemy, a blasphemy, however, bringing light and freedom. The terms of the dogma are a little antiquated now, but it would be easy to re-state them in modern language. For "God" we might substitute "nature and man" or, if we were metaphysically inclined, "God in nature and man." The authors of the Shorter Cate-chism, entangled as they were in a gloomy the-ology, recognized that the significance of life cannot reside in the labor by which men main-tain it, but in some kind of realization of our-

selves and of the world which is the highest
enjoyment conceivable of both.

Let us go back for a few decades and see if we
can catch the values of our time confusedly shaping themselves within the framework of human
life. I say shaping themselves, for as Nietzsche
said fifty years ago, the time of the conscious
valuers has passed; our values for a century
have not been created, they have happened.
They happened because men had become skeptical not merely of God, or of the existence of a
moral order, but of life itself, and could not set
before themselves any purpose justifying life,
but only its bare mechanism, work, duty, the
preservation of society. It has been, thus, one
of the main achievements of modern thought to
banish from the world the notion of enjoyment.
This was begun first in a philosophical way by
the utilitarians, who were reasonably convinced
that, factories existing for the first time as far
as they knew in history, it was incumbent on men
to work in them. A fine philosophy, truly; yet
men believed in it. After the utilitarians came
the advocates of self-help, who showed that the
utilitarian policy might not be without indi-

vidual advantage; that if one cut off one's pleasures, or at least those which cost money, one might win a bizarre, undreamed-of success. The anchorites of wealth arose, the great men who, when they had acquired riches which might have built a new Florence, if scarcely a new Jerusalem, could make no use of them, preferring to teach in Sunday-schools and endow universities. In the eyes of these men wealth was justified only if it could not be enjoyed, for enjoyment was the one thing which went against all their ideas, all those instincts which had set them where they stood. Wealth, thus, could not be enjoyed, could not be used, for when they had reached their end the means still remained means.

The disciples of Smiles have disappeared; men get rich in other ways now; nevertheless a whole view of life has been left behind which we have not fundamentally questioned. The Victorians established the basis of morals in utility; we have come to the stage when we imagine that the basis of life itself is utility. For recreation as an end in itself we have so little appreciation that even sport has become a kind of duty, and nothing is more devastating than the scorn of a conscientious athlete for those who, enjoying perfectly good health, do not go to the trouble of keeping themselves fit. A little unpremeditated pleasure still persists in our common lives, in fox-trotting, drinking, and revues, but it is without either taste or resource; it is not expression but simply relaxation, an amusing way of being tired. The one thing that people will not pardon is the taking of pleasure seriously as an end in itself. The æsthete, at the Renaissance a type of the opulence of life, and quite a common, indeed an expected type, is in our day an aberration demanding our satire when once we have overcome our indignation. Nothing shows more disastrously how incapable we are of entertaining the conviction that life in itself, apart from the labor necessary to make it possible, is a thing worth living. Even art has justified itself for several decades chiefly by its social utility, and only now, against strong opposition, is it escaping from the barriers set up by the generation overawed by Mr. Shaw and Mr. Wells. The notion that men may be on the earth for something else than sweating is dead.

We have arrived at an amazing incapacity for joy; and life is to us always less worth living than it should be.

This exaltation of means has brought about a general instrumentalization of life. It weighs heavily upon men; but upon women its weight is crushing, for women have not such a ready capacity as men for transforming themselves to the image of their functions, and they disfigure themselves more in the attempt. Consequently, as woman has taken a large and larger part in our tentative and unsatisfactory civilization she has undergone, in fact and in people's minds, a distorting process. It is true, woman, lovely woman, the fair charmer, has passed away; but we are hardly better off now when she has become a term like economics. After the economic man has come the economic woman; that is, an entity almost as useful as machinery, and for the inner culture of mankind almost as uninteresting.

How, in striving for emancipation, woman has reached such a dismal stage in her development is one of the saddest stories of our time. The age is an age of work; woman desires freedom,

the right of every human being; and freedom
in such an age can only mean the freedom to
work. But to work, except in a few vocations
such as art, is in our time to specialize oneself,
and the freedom of women has necessarily re-
solved itself into a permission to do little things
which can give them no final satisfaction. Their
freedom is bounded by the slavery under which
men, too, suffer; and in changing their occupations they have not escaped from the cage, but
only out of one compartment of it into another,
a little more cheerless than the first. They have
achieved a little more liberty than they had before; but this liberty is disenchanting because
it leaves them as far away as ever from the full
liberty of their spirit. Perhaps in no other age
has woman been, in a deep, instinctive sense, so
skeptical as she is at present.

And for all this the age—an age in which
labor has a fantastic prominence—is responsible; for it is in a time when everybody works,
and when there is nothing conceivable that one
can do but work, that the cantankerous question
of inequality arises. Only in a race can one be
slower than another; only then does the neces-

sity to become as good a runner as the fastest
come home poignantly to every one.   But if it
should happen that life is not a race at all?
Where leisure is regarded as a more important
thing than work and work falls into its proper,
subordinate place as the mere means to leisure
one does not think very much about inequality,
for it has no longer any urgent importance.   Nor
does one set much value, except in superficials,
on uniformity.   Among people free from crushing labor (as the whole human race may some
time be) there has always been delight in diversity and scorn for uniformity; for, to people
enjoying their spirit and the world, diversity
even when it is exasperating is of infinite interest, giving a satisfying sense of the richness of
life.

Comedy—and comedy is idleness tolerantly
enjoying itself—is founded, it has been said,
upon a recognition of the equality of the sexes;
but it would be more just to say that it is founded
upon a view of life into which the notions of
equality and inequality do not enter at all, because they are unnecessary.   To Congreve and
Stendhal women were not the inferior sex, for,

in spite of the conventions in which ostensibly they moved, they were free, and therefore interesting. And remote as these figures are from us, they demonstrate a very useful truth, that the way to get over our stupid obsession with inequality is to reach a stage where diversity will be the norm, involving disadvantage to no one. Toward that stage, which can only be made possible by a more general leisure, we are moving, if what the reformers and the scientists tell us is true. It will be a stage in which rules will have more importance than laws and spontaneous actions than obligations; and most of the things we do will be regarded as play rather than duty. Conduct will probably be about a fourth of life, instead of the three-fourths postulated by Matthew Arnold. And although this state has not come yet and may not come for a long time, it would be as sensible to found a philosophy upon it as upon a period of transition as dismal and impermanent as ours. Moreover the values of the past are against us as well as those of the future which we imagine. There is a certain ignobility in the dispute over human inequality, a failure to rise to the human level. It is not a question but a misunderstanding, which the accumulated imaginative culture of the world might have made impossible. A little sense of the richness of life would disperse it. Who would be so fantastic as to say that Falstaff is greater or less than Ophelia, or whether Uncle Toby is the exact equal of Anna Karenina? To ask the question is to evoke at once an image of the diverse riches of human nature and of the poverty of mind which can reduce it to such terms, destroying all interest and all nuance.

But where our instrumental philosophy has had the most grotesque effect has been upon our conception of love. People have come to regard love as merely a device for propagating the race. Now this view of love is not new; it has always been dear to the bourgeoisie, who have always thought it a matter of immense moment that they should have sons to carry on their businesses when they were dead. It is the immemorial philistine conception of love: the strange thing is that it has been taken over by the intelligentsia and glorified. This is in the strictest sense a revolution in thought. No one who has written beautifully of love has thought of it as the intellectuals think. To Plato and Dante the essence of love did not reside in procreation; nor has procreation been anything but a divine accident to the poets. And that is in the human tradition, and probably in the natural order of things; for it is possible that both love and procreation are most perfect when they are unpremeditated, and the child comes as a gift and a surprise; for in the fruits of joy there is a principle of exuberance which distinguishes them from the fruits of duty.

The intellectuals have destroyed the humanistic conception of love as pure spontaneity, as expression, by setting its justification not within itself, but in the child. In "Man and Superman" Mr. Shaw makes Tanner say that if our love did not produce another human being to serve the community, the community would have the sacred right of killing us off, just as the hive kills off the drones who do not attain the queen bee. But what does that mean? It means that happiness is of no importance, that it is a matter of the slightest moment whether, in a life which will never be given to us again, we realize some of the potentialities of our being or pass through it blind to the end.   If it is worth while living at all, this must needs be the precise opposite of the truth.   The child, like everything else, is justified; but it is not justified because it adds to the potential wealth of society, but because it adds to our present delight, and moreover lives a life as valid as our own.   The truth is that we dare not admit that any pleasure whatever has a right to exist without serving society, and serving it deliberately.   The joys of other generations have become our duties; and it is significant that Mr. Shaw and the bulk of the intelligentsia are at one on the birth-rate with the Roman Catholic Church, that church which has on many occasions through its theologians affirmed its belief that sensual love is a guilty thing, and, using its own kind of logic, has exhorted man to multiply and replenish the earth.

"The chief end of man is to glorify God and enjoy Him forever"; and that being so, it is the task of those who are a little more serious than the serious to set about discovering the principles of glory and enjoyment in life.   And—I am setting down a truism—the main principle of enjoyment for the human race is not art, nor thought, nor the practice of virtue, but for man, woman, and for woman, man. The exchange of happiness between the sexes is not only the creative agent in human life, perpetuating it; it is also the thing which gives the perpetuation of life its chief meaning. People have always felt this vaguely; it has made labor endurable to them; but hardly ever have they recognized it clearly, and to the poets and artists who know it they have always responded a little skeptically. They have thought of love as a justification a little too materialistic for life; but love is only materialistic when it is regarded as a means.

To accept men and women as ends in themselves, to enter into their life as one of them, is to partake of absolute life, that life which at every moment realizes itself, existing for its own sake. We cannot live in that life continuously; for the accomplishment of the intricate purposes of society we must at certain times and with part of our minds regard our fellow-creatures as instruments; but the more we tend to do so the more we banish joy from life. Life does not consist, whatever the utilitarians may say, in functioning, but in living; and life comes into being where men and women, not as functions, but as self-constituted entities, intersect. This is the state which in religion as well as art has been called life; this is the final life of the earth, beyond which there is no other. We may accept it or pass it by; but whatever we may do with it, it is our chief end, giving meaning to the multitudinous pains of humanity. This commerce between men and women is not merely sexual, in the narrow sense which we have given the word; it involves every human joy, all the thoughts and aspirations of mankind stretching into infinity. It is the thing which has inspired all great artists, mystical as well as earthy. It is the point of reference for any morality which is not a disguised kind of adaptation; for virtue consists in the capacity to partake freely of human happiness. All reform, all economic and political theory has a meaning in so far as it makes for this; and that was recognized by the first reformers, the utopians who had not yet become mere specialists in reform.

The libertarian movement has been such a dismal affair, thus, not because it has been too free, but because it has not been free enough. The democracies and the women of the world have been potentially liberated; but not so very long ago they were slaves, and they have still a slave's idea of freedom. Instead of equal joys they have asked for equal obligations; and the whole world is in the grip of a psychological incapacity to escape from the idea of obligation. Against the unreasonable solemnity which this has imposed on everything there is little left for us except a deliberate and reasonable light-heartedness; this, and the faith that the human race will some time attain the only kind of freedom worth striving for, a freedom in joy.

Virtue for Women
By Isabel Leavenworth

Isabel Leavenworth

is an instructor in philosophy at Barnard College.

VIRTUE FOR WOMEN

BY ISABEL LEAVENWORTH

IN the turmoil of discussion regarding present modes of sex life one can discern a pretty general approval of just one element in the whole situation: the ideal by which the good woman has for so long been controlled. It is commonly held that if changes are to be made they should be in the direction of persuading men, and also the few women who have been at fault, to be just as good as our good women have always been. Thus the young girl of to-day is criticized on the ground that instead of raising men to her level she is descending to theirs. Even those who are inclined to belittle the damage which she is doing to the social structure accompany their mild defense with the consoling reminder that human nature does not change and that in the end the girl of to-day will turn out as well as did the girls of yesterday; that is, she will finally come around to the good old feminine way of doing things.

It seems to me most unfortunate that the majority of people hope to improve matters through an extension of the feminine ideals of the past. In the established scheme of things one finds a peculiarly gross form of immorality, an immorality incommensurably greater than the dreaded evil of promiscuity; and it is only as an element in this total scheme that woman's ideals have any significance. The fact that they have always constituted one side of a "double standard" is not merely something which may be said about their relation to other elements after their essential characteristics have been considered. These characteristics can be described only in terms of the double standard and of its attendant evils. It would be as impossible, then, to destroy the double standard and still keep the feminine ideal intact as it would be to preserve the convex nature of a mathematical curve while destroying the concave. According to the present system there is a standard of conduct set up for women which is to constitute virtue. This standard is a combination of specific positive

commands and, more especially, of specific prohibitions. There are certain things which no
nice woman will do—a great many things, in
fact. She must learn them by heart and accept
them on faith as the Pythagoreans must have had
to learn their curious list of taboos, a list running from the taboo against eating beans to that
against sitting on a quart measure. This ideal of
virtue does not apply with equal rigidity to men;
quite different things are expected of them and
accepted for them. It is obvious that two
such conflicting ideals by the very nature of their
combination will produce a class of women who
do not live up to the standard of virtue set them
as members of their sex. This class is not merely
an excrescence but an integral part of the situation created by the total sex ideal of society. The
function of women of this class is to make possible for men the way of life commonly considered as suited to their sex and to make possible
a virtuous life for the remainder of womankind.
In fulfilling this function such women lose, in
the eyes of society, their moral nature and forfeit
the right to live within the pale of social morality. They are considered unfit for normal so-

cial intercourse and are denied those relationships and responsibilities which ordinarily serve
as the basis for moral growth. From all normal
responsibility toward them society regards itself
as released. That which is personal, the inner
life, the character, the soul—whatever one prefers to call it—having been sacrificed in the
service of the social scheme, one is to treat what
is left as of no value in itself, but merely
as an instrument to be used in the service of
man's pleasure or woman's virtue. The prostitute is to society that one thing, defined by the
purpose which she serves, and that is all she is,
all she is allowed to be. The depersonalization,
the moral non-existence, one might call it, of a
large number of women is, then, implicit in the
social system currently accepted. It is not a
punishment meted out to those who fail to act in
accordance with the social scheme (though it is
as such, of course, that society defends it) but is
itself an absolutely essential element in the social
scheme, an element woven in and out through the
entire fabric of current sex morality.

It is curious how many people feel that a
choice between the present system and any other

is reducible to a choice between different degrees of promiscuity. Promiscuity would be an evil, but it does not in itself involve this particular immorality. The worst evils in the present situation are due not to the "lower" half of the double standard but to the doubleness itself.

It is true that the ideal of womanly virtue is only one element in the conventional system of sex morality. But, like a Leibnitzian monad, it reflects the whole universe within itself—the universe of sex mores. It is in no real sense any "higher" than the ideal by which men have lived. They are warp and woof of the same fabric. According to this ideal it is woman's prime duty to keep aloof from evil. This sounds commendable enough. And it would be at least innocuous if one could interpret it as meaning that woman should hold herself aloof from some imagined evil that would become existent were she to embrace it. This is not, however, a possible interpretation of the varied collection of prohibitions which it is her duty to respect. Their import is clearly enough that she is to keep aloof from evil which is already existent, which is an acknowledged part of her background. She is to shun all of those vulgarities, coarsenesses, and immoralities which are to enter into the lives of men and for which, one is forced to conclude, the "other" women are to provide. And from this other class of women she is, of course, to keep herself absolutely separate, distinct. I recently heard an elderly Boston lady make a remark which expresses the horror commonly aroused by any conduct which endangers the distinction between the two classes. "Do you know," she said, "I heard that a young man of our set said he and his friends no longer had to go to girls of another kind for their enjoyment. They can get all they want from girls of their own class." This was the outrage. The nice girls were allowing the classes to become confused. Much the same attitude is revealed in the frequent remark that the young girl of to-day appears like "any chorus girl" or like any "common woman." The horrid picture is usually rounded off with the comment that you simply can't tell the difference any more between the nice girl and the other kind. One can imagine that this might cause considerable inconvenience. Each of the two classes of women has served a special purpose and it is, to say the least, disconcerting for a person not to know which way to turn when he knows very well which purpose he wants fulfilled.

The precautions which a good woman takes to preserve her purity are indeed legion. There are places where no nice woman will go, situations with which she must have no immediate acquaintance, people with whom she must not associate; there are various embodiments of evil, in short, to which she must not expose herself. That these evils should exist, that they should be tolerated as meeting certain needs in the lives of men and be made possible by other women— all this the average good woman swallows without repulsion, or, more commonly, ignores. She is aroused to a state of true indignation only when her own moral exclusiveness, or that of her kind, is threatened. The same woman who accepts with a good deal of equanimity the fact that men she associates with also associate with "gay" women would be considerably upset if these men were to attempt to associate with both kinds of women at the same time. Why is the average woman so upset if a man of her acquaintance makes "improper advances"? Is it that she is horrified to find that he is willing to indulge his irregular sex desires? No. She is outraged because he thinks she is willing to indulge hers, because he holds her virtue too lightly. Sex evils, coarsenesses are then to be part of the good woman's environment in the intimate sense that they often enter into the lives of the men she accepts as friends, even of the men with whom she is to have the most personal and supposedly ideal relationships. Her sole function is to turn her back on these evils. The point of prime importance to her is that they should not pollute her; and the first demand which she makes upon men is that they shall show their respect for this ideal by keeping her apart.

The acceptance of this situation is implied in the ideals which are passed down to girls by the good old-fashioned parent. Do the mothers who insist that their daughters shall not go with boys on certain occasions and at certain hours unchaperoned expect boys to refrain from seeing any girls except on occasions thus carefully timed and adequately supervised? I doubt it. Whatever their expectations may be, it is certain that they would rather that the good girl should cling to protection, letting the man seek gayety where he may, than that she should take the chance involved in seeking gayety by his side. They would rather have what they consider the evil sex element taken care of by men and by a class of women devoted by society to that purpose than to risk any slip in conduct on the part of their own daughters. Purity purchased at such a price may be purity in some magical sense, similar to that secured in the ancient mysteries by passing through fire or going in bathing with sacred pigs. Purity in any moral sense it certainly is not. It is simply a social asset, like physical beauty or pleasing accomplishments, so tremendously valuable to woman that for it she has been willing to pay any moral price, however degrading. Its non-moral character is revealed in the common assumption that any man can, without injury to himself, pass through experiences or be placed in situations from which, since they would pollute her, every good woman must be guarded. This assumption, so obviously insulting to women, is at present complacently accepted by them as something of a compliment.

William Graham Sumner in his remarkably unemotional and objective treatment of social customs devotes some pages to a description of the houses of prostitution established and run by the cities of medieval Europe "in the interest of virtuous women." In this connection Mr. Sumner for once indulges in terms of opprobrium, judging the custom as "the most incredible case" illustrating "the power of the mores to extend toleration and sanction to an evil thing." The inmates of these houses were dedicated entirely to this special function, wore distinctive dress, and were taboo to all "good" women whose virtue, according to the scheme of things, they made possible. Authority for such a custom can be found, as Sumner points out, in Saint Augustine, the reformed rake. "The bishop," writes Sumner, "has laid down the proposition that evil things in human society, under the great orderly scheme of things which he was trying to expound, are overruled to produce good." Is not this the position taken by people who hold that it is better to have prostitution in order to provide for the assumed sex

irregularity of men than to risk the loss of a
woman's "virtue" through the removal of those
conventions and taboos which prevent her from
coping with the situation herself and making her
own moral decisions? I can see no difference.
Has man at any period of his checkered moral
career devised a more unpleasant method of sav-
ing his own soul? The good woman sits serenely
on the structure upheld for her by prostitutes
and occasionally even commits the absurdity of
attempting to "reform" these women, the necessity for whose existence is implied by the beliefs
according to which she herself lives.

It is hard to follow the mental processes of
those persons who, while deploring the increased
freedom allowed women and the tendency to
judge them less severely, still claim belief in a
single standard for both sexes. In so far as woman's virtue consists in aloofness from the evils
which the double standard implies it quite obviously cannot be adopted as the single standard
by which all members of society are to live.
Even aside from this consideration it would seem
to be as undesirable as it is impossible to extend
to men the traditions and restrictions which have

for so long governed women. Does any one really wish to have grown boys constantly accompanied and watched over by their elders? Does any one wish that the goings and comings of men should be as specifically determined as those of women have always been? Should we look forward to a day when a man will be judged as good or bad on the sole basis of whether or not he has ever had any irregular sex relation?

One would think that the suspicions of even the most uncritical might be aroused by the rigidly absolute and impersonal nature of women's sex ideals. The notion of purity as lying in the abstention from a particular act except under carefully prescribed circumstances has all the marks of a primitive taboo and none of the characteristics of a rational moral principle. The ideals of woman's honor and chastity have without doubt been built up in answer to human wants—the defense which is invariably given of customs, good or bad. Probably those sociologists are not far wrong who hold that they have developed as a response, in early times, to the sentiments of man as a property owner; later, in response to masculine vanity and jealousy, though these motives have, of course, been idealized beyond all recognition. We need not be surprised, then, to find that they bear no relation to an interest in woman's spiritual welfare and growth, an interest to which society is only now giving birth with pitiable pains of labor. To follow an ideal which almost entirely excludes sex interest as something evil is to condemn one of the richest elements in personal experience. And this ideal has regulated not only woman's sex experience but has demanded and received incalculable sacrifices in all the phases of her life, mercilessly limiting the sphere of her activities, smothering interests of value and nourishing others to an unnatural state of development, and warping her character to satisfy its most exacting demands. Because she must first of all conform to an unpolluted archetype, and because society must be secure in the knowledge that she is indeed so conforming, she has never been able to meet life freely, to make what experience she could out of circumstances, to poke about here and there in the nooks and crannies of her surroundings better to understand the world in which she lives. We find here a more subtle but more deadly limitation than exclusion from institutions of learning or from political privileges. And under this limitation woman has labored in the service of a paltry ideal.

Not only is it undesirable that men should attempt to follow such an ideal but it is quite obvious that as long as they accept it as adequate for women they are prevented in innumerable ways from developing intelligent principles for their own guidance. For one thing, they will come to look upon the sex element in most of its forms as a moral evil. Experience tells them, however, that it is, in their own case, a natural good. Thus they are led to accept a distinction fatal to moral integrity and progress. The sex element is admitted to the life of the average man by the back door; once within, it has fair run of the establishment though it is always looked on askance by the other members of the household. Sex interests are to be recognized and indulged but divorced from all that is "fine" and "ideal." They are considered desirable though immoral and so are to be tolerated just to the extent that they are divorced from those elements in society—the family, the home, and good women—which are supposed to embody virtue. It is not realized that virtue, far from being a rival of the other good things of life, is to be attained only through an intelligent interest in good things, and that to divorce moral from natural good is to deal a death blow to both. We cannot wonder that at present sex interest so often expresses itself in the form of dubious stories, coarse revues, and degrading physical relations. While the "good" woman who considers sex somehow lowering is apt to develop a personality which is anemic and immature, the man who accepts the conventional scheme of life develops a personality coarse and uncoördinated.

I do not mean to say that there have been no elements of value in the ideal of purity by which some women have lived. It is undoubtedly true that unregulated and impersonal sex desires and activities quarrel with more stable and fruitful interests in life. But while the most valuable experiences of love are, in general, to be found in more lasting relations, it does not follow that society should prescribe for every one of its members a particular line of sex conduct and attempt to see, through constant supervision, that its prescriptions are carried out. The sacrifice in terms of freedom of activity and experience is too great and the living flower of personal purity cannot be manufactured by any such artificial methods.

The sex relations of an individual should no more be subjected to social regulation than his friendships. There is indeed a closely related matter for which he is immediately responsible to society—that is the welfare of any children resulting from such relations. The two matters are, however, quite distinguishable and no one could hold that the effort which society makes to control sex relations is to any extent based upon concern for the welfare of possible offspring. If this were so, one would not hear so much condemnation of birth-control measures on the ground that they "encourage immorality." No. It is personal experience which society would like to prescribe for its members, personal virtue that it would like to mold for them. But virtue is not a predetermined result, a kind of spiritual dessert that any one can cook up who will follow with due care the proper ethical receipt. It is,

on the contrary, something which is never twice
alike; something which appears in ever new and
lovely forms as the fruit of harmoniously developed elements in a unique character complex.
Experience cannot be defined in terms of external circumstances and bodily acts and thus
judged as absolutely good or bad. Sex experiences, like other experiences, can be judged of
only on the basis of the part which they play in
the creative drama of the individual soul. There
are as many possibilities for successful sex life as
there are men and women in the world. A significant single standard can be attained only
through the habit of judging every case, man or
woman, in the light of the character of the individual and of the particular circumstances in
which he or she is placed.

From the changes taking place in sex morality
we may, with sufficient wisdom and courage, win
inestimable gains. Certainly we should be grate-
ful that young people are forming the habit of
meeting this old problem in a quite new way—
that is, with the coöperation of the two sexes. In
the interest of this newer approach we should

accord to girls as much freedom from immediate supervision as we have always given to boys. The old restrictions, imposed upon girls alone, imply, of course, the double standard with all its attendant evils; imply the placid acceptance of two essentially different systems of value; imply the preference for physical purity over personal responsibility and true moral development. We should encourage the daughters of to-day in their fast developing scorn for the "respect" which our feminine predecessors thought was their due —a respect which man was expected to reveal in the habit of keeping the nice woman untouched by certain rather conspicuous elements, interests, and activities in his own life. In so far as there is something truly gay in these aspects of life, something which men know at the bottom of their hearts they should not be called on to forego, there is much that women can learn. Most people to-day hold in their minds an image of two worlds—one of gayety and freedom, the other of morality. It is because gayety and morality are thus divorced that gayety becomes sordidness, morality dreariness. Not until men and women develop together the legitimate interests which both of these worlds satisfy will the present inconsistency and hypocrisy be done away with and both men and women be free to achieve, if they can, rich and unified personal lives.

Where Are the Female Geniuses?
By Sylvia Kopald

Sylvia Kopald

*is primarily a specialist in labor and the author of
a recent study of outlaw strikes, "Rebellion in
Labor Unions."*

WHERE ARE THE FEMALE GENIUSES?

BY SYLVIA KOPALD

MANY years ago, Voltaire was initiated into the mysteries of Newton by Mme. du Châtelet. Finishing her translation and her rich commentary upon the *Principles,* in a glow he extended to her the greatest tribute which man has yet found for exceptional women. He said, "A woman who has translated and illuminated Newton is, in short, a very great man." Genius has long been a masculine characteristic, although some more generous authors admit its possession by certain "depraved" women. Only the courtesans of classical antiquity could be women and individuals at once, and, therefore, Jean Finot found it necessary to remind us emphatically even in 1913 that "women of genius and talent are not necessarily depraved." Not necessarily, mind you. No, the great woman may be, in short, a great man, but she is not necessarily depraved.

As the twentieth century progresses and women capture the outposts of individuality one after the other, the old questions lose much of their old malignancy. Women battle with the problem of how to combine a home and a career and men become less sure (especially in these days of high living costs) that woman's place is in the home. As women enter the trades and the arts and the professions, men begin to discover comrades where there were only girls and wives and mothers before. It is an exciting century, this women's century, and even though prejudices crumble slowly, they crumble. Yet one of the old questions remains, stalwart and unyielding as ever: Where are the female geniuses?

Even a pessimist may find cause for rejoicing in this final wording of the "woman question." Man's search for the female genius is more consoling than his sorrowful quest for the snows of yesteryear. For snows, like all beauty, have a way of melting with time; a mind ripens and mellows with age. Granted a mind which it is no longer a shame or a battle to develop, women can look upon the passing of the years with at least as great an equanimity as does man. She remains in the picture of life long after the Maker's paints have begun to dry. And that is good. But as long as the female geniuses remain undiscovered, it must be also a bit insecure. Women may have minds—every average man will now grant that. But (he will quickly ask) have they ever much more than average minds? Look at history, which this time really does prove what you want it to. Every high peak in the historic landscape is masculine. Point them out just as they occur to you: Shakespeare, Dante, Goethe, Virgil, Horace, Catullus, Plato, Socrates, Newton, Darwin, Pasteur, Watt, Edison, Steinmetz, Heine, Shelley, Keats, Beethoven, Wagner, Bach, Tolstoi. . . .

Where are the *female* geniuses?

It has really become much more than a question of feminist conversation. Science has attempted to put its seal of approval upon the implied answer to this rhetorical question. It has sought to put the notion that "a woman is only a woman, but a genius is a man," into impressively scientific lingo. The argument goes something like this: In regard to practically all anatomical, physiological, and psychic characteristics, the male exhibits a greater variability (i.e. a greater range of spreading down from and up above the average) than the female. The male is the agent of variation; the female is the agent of type conservation. This sex difference operates in the realm of mental ability as everywhere. In any comparable group of men and women, the distribution of intelligence will tend to follow the law of chances (Gaussian Curve). But female intelligence will cluster far more about its average than male. There will be more imbeciles and idiots among men, but there will also be more geniuses. It is really very simple, as the following arbitrary example will show. Supposing you take comparable sample groups of 1000 men and 1000 women from a given population. After testing them for grade of intelligence, you classify them according to previously accepted "intelligence classes." Your results would tend to read a little like this:

Intelligence Class	Number Men	Number Women
Idiots	10	3
Inferior	100	50
Slow	200	150
Average	380	595
Able	200	150
Highly Talented	100	52
Geniuses	10	..

Of course none of the proponents of this theory would state the alleged facts of man's greater variability in such bald terms. But all of them would agree that men do vary more than women and in some such fashion. In this greater variability they see the explanation of men's monopoly of genius.

According to Karl Pearson this "law of the greater variability of the male" was first stated by Darwin. Somewhat earlier, the anatomist Meckel had concluded that the female is more variable than the male. It is interesting to note in passing that he consequently judged "variation a sign of inferiority." By the time Burdach, Darwin, and others had declared the male more variable, however, variation had become an advantage and the basis and hope of all progress. To-day great social significance is attached to the comparative variability of the sexes, especially in its application to the questions of sex differences in mental achievement. Probably the outstanding English-speaking supporters of the theory in its modern form have been Havelock Ellis and Dr. G. Stanley Hall. But even so cautious a student as Dr. E. L. Thorndike has granted it his guarded support. And Dr. James McKeen Cattell has explained the results of his study of 1000 eminent characters of history by means of it. Indeed many others hold the theory in one form or another—e.g. Münsterburg, Patrick. What is most important, of course, is that its supporters do not stop with the mere statement of the theory. They ascribe to it tremendous effects in the past and ask for it a large influence in the shaping of our policies in the present.

For Havelock Ellis, the greater variability of the male "has social and practical consequences of the widest significance. The whole of our human civilization would have been a different thing if in early zoölogical epochs the male had not acquired a greater variational tendency than the female." ("Man and Woman," p. 387.) Professor Hall builds up upon it a scheme of gushingly paradisaical (and properly boring) education for the adolescent girl, which "keeps the purely mental back" and develops the soul, the body, and the intuitions. ("The Psychology of Adolescence," Vol. II, Chap. 17.) Just because Professor Thorndike is so careful in his statements, his practical deductions from the theory are most interesting: "Thus the function of education for women, though not necessarily differentiated by the small differences in average capacity, is differentiated by the difference in range of ability. Not only the probability and desirability of marriage and the training of children as an essential feature of women's career but also the restriction of women to the mediocre grades of ability and achievement should be reckoned with by our educational systems. The education of women for such professions as administration, statesmanship, philosophy, or scientific research, where a few very gifted individuals are what society requires, is far less needed than education for such professions as nursing, teaching, medicine, or architecture, where the average level is essential. Elementary education is probably an even better investment for the community in the case of girls than in the case of boys; for almost all girls profit by it, whereas the extremely low grade boy may not be up to his school education in zeal or capacity and the extremely high grade boy may get on better without it. So also with high school education. On the other hand, post graduate instruction to which women are flocking in great numbers is, at least in its higher reaches, a far more remunerative social investment in the case of men." ("Sex in Education," *Bookman*, Vol. XXIII, April, 1906, p. 213.)

Before we begin the revision of our educational systems in accordance with this theory, we must make sure that it really explains away the "female geniuses." For although the theory is still widely held by biologists and psychologists, it requires only a short study to discover how tenuous is the evidence adduced in support of it —in all its phases, but especially in regard to mental traits. Darwin apparently gave no statistical evidence to support "the principle," as he called it, and those who have followed him have done little to fill the lack. Professor Hall offers evidence that is almost entirely empirical; Havelock Ellis has been attacked by Karl Pearson for doing much "to perpetuate some of the worst of the pseudo-scientific superstitions to which he [Ellis] refers, notably that of the greater variability of the male human being." Professor Thorndike, in spite of his conclusions, admits that it "is unfortunate that so little information is available for a study of sex differences in the variability of mental traits in the case of individuals over fifteen." And while the overwhelming majority of Professor Cattell's 1000 eminent characters are men, he merely states without proving his explanation that "woman departs less from the normal than man."

Wise feminists to-day are concentrating their forces upon this theory. Women have won the right to an acknowledged mind; they want now the right to draw for genius and high talents in the "curve of chance." And this is no merely academic question. For while genius may overcome the sternest physical barriers of environment, it is nourished and developed by tolerant expectancy. Men may accomplish anything, popular thought tells them, and so some men do. But if women are scientifically excluded from the popular expectation of big things, if their educations are toned down to preparation for "the average level," if motherhood remains the *only* respected career for *all* women, then the female geniuses will remain few and far between. And, more important still, all thinking women will continue restless over the problem of how to secure the chance to vary in interests and abilities from the average of their sex, and at the same time to be wives and mothers.

In this fight for a full chance to compete, woman may do one (or all) of three things. She may merely ignore the theory and go on "working and living," trusting that as environmental barriers fall one after the other, this final question, too, will lose its meaning. She can point out in support of this attitude that the past does contain its female geniuses, however few; and certainly if all the barriers that have been set up against woman's entry into the larger world have not entirely stifled female genius, we may at least look forward hopefully to a kinder future. Something of this attitude, of this demand for free experimentation, must make part of every woman's armor against the implications of this theory. But taken alone, it becomes more merely defensive than the status of the theory deserves. For it is really the theory that must defend itself. It must not only bring forward more affirmative evidence, but it must also meet the contrary findings of such investigation as has been made. It must, again, prove its title to *the cause* of the scarcity of female geniuses when so many other more eradicable causes may be at its bottom.

The actual evidence that has been gathered on this question is still uncertain and fragmentary. While it does not yet establish anything definitely, it points to rather surprising conclusions. In all cases investigated the discovered differences in variability have been very slight, and if they balance either way tend to prove a greater variability among women. Neither sex need have a monopoly of either imbeciles or geniuses, but women may yet be found to be slightly more favored with both!

The first painstaking investigation in this field was made by Dr. Karl Pearson who published his interesting results as one essay in his *Chances of Death and Other Studies in Evolution* in 1897. Under the heading "Variation in Man and Woman" (Vol. I, pp. 256-377), written as a polemical attack upon Havelock Ellis's stand in this theory, he set forth results of measurements upon men and women in seventeen anatomical characteristics. He obtained his data from statistics already collected, from measurements of living men and women, and from post-mortem and archeological examinations. Female variability (coefficients of variation) proved greater in eleven of these seventeen characteristics, male in six. He concluded among other things that "there is . . . no evidence of greater male variability, but rather of a slightly greater female variability. Accordingly the principle that man is more variable than woman must be put on one side as a pseudo-scientific superstition until it has been demonstrated in a more scientific manner than has hitherto been attempted."

To round out this evidence Doctors Leta Hollingworth and Helen Montague measured 20,000 infants at their birth in the maternity wards of the New York Infirmary for Women and Children. They sought to discover whether environmental influences played any determining rôle in producing the results obtained by Pearson from measurements upon adults. From the ten anatomical measurements made upon these babies they found that "in all cases the differences in variability are very slight. In only two cases does the percentile variation differ in the first decimal place. In these two cases the variability is once greater for males and once greater for females." ("The Comparative Variability of the Sexes at Birth," *American Journal of Sociology,* Vol. XX, 1914-1915, pp. 335-370.)

The findings on anatomical variability do not, of course, necessarily prove anything about differences in the range of mental ability. They do, however, suggest the probability of parallel results and such studies as have been made tend, on the whole, to bear this out. All the recent work in this field (and it is still fragmentary) seems to point at least to equal mental variability among men and women. In 1917, Terman and others in their "Stanford Revision of the Binet-Simon Scale for Measuring Intelligence" investigated this problem among school children from five to fourteen years old. They obtained the Intelligence Quotients of 457 boys and 448 girls and compared these I.Q.'s with teachers' estimates and judgments of intelligence and work and with the age grade distribution of the sexes for the ages of 7 to 14. After making all necessary qualifications, they concluded that the tests revealed a small superiority in the intelligence of the girls that "probably rests upon a real superiority in intelligence, age for age." But "apart from the small superiority of the girls, the distribution of intelligence shows no significant differences in the sexes. The data offer no support to the wide-spread belief that girls group themselves more closely about the median or that extremes of intelligence are more common among boys" (p. 83).

Dr. Hollingworth, again, has made a study of mental differences for adults. She has summarized the results of recent studies in sex differences in mental variability and in tastes, perceptions, interests, etc. Her conclusions on this score are interesting: "(1) The greater variability of males in anatomical traits is not established, but is debated by authorities of perhaps equal competence. (2) But even if it were established, it would only suggest, not prove, that men are more variable in mental traits also. The empirical data at present available on this point are inadequate and contradictory, and if they point either way, actually indicate greater female variability. . . ." ("Variability as Related to Sex Differences in Achievement," *American Journal of Sociology,* Vol. XIX, pp. 510-530, Jan., 1914.)

It seems hardly safe scientifically, therefore, to restrict women to the average levels in education and work and profession on the ground that eminence is beyond their range. But if the female geniuses have not been cut off by a comparatively narrowed range of mental ability, where are they? Certainly history does not reveal them in anything like satisfactory number. And it is now that women may bring forward their third weapon of attack. The female geniuses may have been missing not because of an inherent lack in the make-up of the sex, but because of the oppressive, restrictive cultural conditions under which women have been forced to live.

The important rôle played by cultural conditions in the cultural achievement of various nations and races has been noted with increasing emphasis by the newer schools of sociology and anthropology. No scholar can now defend unchallenged a thesis of "lower or higher races" by urging the achievements of any race as an index of its range of mental ability. Culture grows by its own laws and the high position of the white race may be as much a product of favorable circumstances as of exceptional innate capacities. Similarly the expression taken by the genius of various nations appears to vary strikingly. This is especially impressive in the realm of music. The Anglo-Saxon peoples are singularly lacking in great musical composers. Neither Britain nor America, nor indeed any of the northern countries have contributed one composer worthy of mention beside the Beethovens and Wagners and Chopins of this art. Indeed the great names in music are generally of German, Latin or Slavic origin. Yet no one thinks of urging this fact as evidence of an Anglo-Saxon failure of major creativeness. Instead we point to achievements in other fields or at most attempt to explain this peculiar lack by some external causation. Similarly all our impatience with the un-artistic approaches of the American people does not lead us to frame a theory of their lack of genius. There are many cultural factors to be considered first.

But as soon as we approach the problem of female genius, too many of us are apt to bring forward an entirely different kind of interpretation.

We pass over the undoubted female geniuses lightly—granting Sappho and Bonheur and Brunn and Eliot and Brontë and Amster and Madame Curie and Caroline Herschel and perhaps even Chaminade and Clara Schumann and several others. We admit the undoubtedly significant parts women are playing in modern literature. But the question always remains.

Yet in no national or racial group have cultural influences exercised so restrictive an influence as among the entire female sex. Not only has the larger world been closed to them, not only has popular opinion assumed that "no woman has it in her," but the bearing and rearing of children has carried with it in the past the inescapable drudgery of housework. And this is "a field," as Dr. Hollingworth points out, "where eminence is not possible."

It was Prudhon who sneered in response to a similar argument that "women could not even invent their distaff." But we now know enough about the laws of invention to realize how unfair such sneering is. Professor Franz Boas and his school have long demonstrated that cultural achievement and mental ability are not necessarily correlated. For material culture, once it begins, tends to grow by accumulation and diffusion. Each generation adds to the existing stock of knowledge, and as the stock grows the harvests necessarily become greater. Modern man need have no greater mental ability than the men of the ice ages to explain why his improvements upon the myriad machines and tools that are his yield so much larger a harvest than the Paleolithic hunters' improvements upon their few flint weapons and industrial processes. For, as Professor Ogburn has well shown (in "Social Change," Part III) all invention contains two elements—a growing cultural base and inventive genius to work with the materials it furnishes. The number of new inventions necessarily grows with the cultural base. Even 50 times 100 make only 5000, but 2 times 1,000,000 make 2,000,000. Countless generations have added their share to the total material culture which is ours and which we shall hand down still more enriched to posterity.

It must be at once obvious that there has been no such cultural growth in housework. Housework has long remained an individualized, noncumulative industry, where daughter learns from mother the old ways of doing things. The small improvements and ingenuities which most housewives devise seldom find their way into the whole stream of culture. Thus it is that the recent great inventions which are slowly revolutionizing this last stronghold of petty individualism have come from the man-made world. Workers in electricity could more easily devise the vacuum cleaner than the solitary housewife; the electric washer, parquet floors, the tin can, quantity production of stockings, wool, clothing, bread, butter, and all the other instruments that have really made possible women's emancipation have naturally come not from women's minds (any more than from men's) but from the growth of culture and the minds that utilize that growth for further expansion.

Consequently, as women participate in the work of the world and win the right to acquire the results of past achievement in science and technique and art, we may expect their contributions to the social advance to appear in ever greater numbers. Until we give them this full chance to contribute, we have no right to explain the paucity of their gifts to society by inherent lacks. And it seems reasonable to expect that such a chance will render the old quest for female geniuses properly old-fashioned. For they will be there, these women—the able and talented and geniuses—working side by side with men, not as "very great men" nor as necessarily "depraved" nor in any way unusual. They will be there as human beings and as women.

Man and Woman as Creators
By Alexander Goldenweiser

Alexander Goldenweiser,

psychologist and anthropologist, is a lecturer at the New School for Social Research in New York.

MAN AND WOMAN AS CREATORS

BY ALEXANDER GOLDENWEISER

"A HEN is no bird, a woman—no human," says a Russian proverb. In this drastic formulation stands written the history of centuries. Woman's claim to "human"ness was at times accepted with reservations, at other times it was boldly challenged and even to-day when woman's legal, social, economic and political disabilities have been largely removed, woman's acceptance in society as man's equal remains dependent on a definition of the "equal."

As in the case of the mental capacity of races, the question of woman's intellectual status was never judged on its merits. Rather, it was accepted as a practical social postulate, then rationalized into the likeness of an inductive conclusion. The problem seems so replete with temptations for special pleading that a thoroughly impartial attitude becomes well-nigh impossible. However, let us attempt it!

Is woman psychologically identical with man? or, if there is a difference, is it one of superiority and inferiority? And of what practical significance is this issue to society?

Two ways of approach are open: subject men and women to psychological tests, or observe performance in life and, exercising due critical care, infer capacity.

Both methods have been tried. The first enjoys to-day a certain vogue: it is the method of science, of experimental psychology. Unfortunately, the findings of science in this field have to date resulted in precisely nothing. It was feasible to assume that woman was man's equal in elementary sensory capacity, in memory, types and varieties of associations, attention, sensitiveness to pain, heat and cold, etc. Experimental psychology has confirmed these assumptions. But what of it? What can we make of it? Precisely nothing. What we are interested in is whether woman can think "as logically" as man, whether she is more intuitive, more emotional, less imaginative, more practical, less honest, more sensitive, a better judge of human nature. These, among many other interesting issues cannot even be broached by experimental psychology "within the present state of our knowledge."

Remains the second method, to observe performance and infer capacity.

To examine in this fashion all the issues involved would require a small library. I select only one, creativeness. Is woman man's equal in creativeness? The choice is justified by the highly controversial character of the issue as well as its practical bearings.

Two periods in the history of civilization lend themselves admirably for our purpose, the primitive and the modern.

The primitive world was not innocent of discrimination against woman. In social and political leadership, in the ownership and disposition of property, in religion and ceremonialism, woman was subjected to more or less drastic restrictions. It would, therefore, be obviously unfair to expect her creativeness in these fields to have equaled or even approximated that of man. Not so in industry and art, where division of labor prevailed, but no sex disability. As one surveys the technical and artistic pursuits of primitive tribes, woman's participation is everywhere in evidence. The baskets of California, the painted pots of the Pueblos, the beaded embroideries of the Plains, the famous Chilkat blankets, the tapa cloth of Polynesia, all of these were woman's handiwork. Almost everywhere she plans and cuts and sews and decorates the garments worn by women as well as men. Also, in all primitive communities she gathers the wild products of vegetation and transforms them into palatable foods. More than this, in societies that know not the plow woman is, with few exceptions, the agriculturist. It follows that the observations, skills, techniques and inventions involved in these pursuits must also be credited to woman.

It will be conceded that in primitive society woman's record is impressive: wherever she is permitted to apply her creativeness she makes good, and the excellence of her achievement is equal to that of man, certainly not conspicuously inferior to his.

In evaluating these findings, however, it is important to take cognizance of the submergence of individual initiative by the tribal pattern, a feature characteristic of primitive life. This applies to men and women, to artisans and artists. Imaginative flights being cut short by traditional norms, the individualism and subjectivism of modern art are here conspicuous by their absence.

How does this record compare with a survey of the modern period?

Here again woman's disabilities in the social, political and religious realms were so marked that creative participation was impossible. The same is true of architecture. Then come philosophy, mathematics, science, and sculpture, painting, literature, music and the drama. In philosophy and mathematics there is no woman in the ranks of supreme excellence. Even Sonya Kovalevsky, though a talent, was not a great mathematician. In science also, where women have done fine things, none are found among the brightest luminaries. It must be added, moreover, that the few women who have made their mark in the scientific field, notably Mme. Curie, have done so in the laboratory, not in the more abstract and imaginative domain of theoretical science.

At this point some may protest that the period

during which women have had a chance to test their talents in philosophy, mathematics and science was too short, their number too small, and that here once more performance cannot fairly be used as a measure of possible achievement. We must heed this protest.

As to sculpture, painting, literature, music and the drama, I claim that woman's protracted disabilities cannot in any way be held accountable for whatever her performance may be found to be. Women artists, musicians, writers and, of course, actresses, have been with us for a long time. Their number is large and on the increase. Whether married or single, they devote their energies to these pursuits quite unhampered by social taboos. There are in this field no taboos against women. In the United States, in fact, these occupations are held to be more suitable for women than for men.

But what do we find?

In painting and sculpture, no women among the best, although considerable numbers among the second best and below. There is no woman Rodin or Meunier or Klinger or Renoir or Picasso.

In literature the case for woman stands better. Here women have performed wonderfully, both in poetry and prose. If they have fallen short, it is only of supreme achievement.*

Finally we come to music and the stage. The case of music is admirably suited for our purpose, is really a perfect test case. What do we find? As performers, where minor creativeness suffices, women have equaled the best among men. As composers, where creativeness of the highest order is essential, they have failed. We have a Carreño or Novaes to match a Hofmann or Levitski, a Melba or Sembrich to match a

* We need not mention a Dante, Shakespeare, Cervantes or Milton. Perhaps these are too far back. Not so Tolstoi, Dostoyevski, Turgenev, Goethe, Heine, Balzac, Maupassant, the Goncourts, Flaubert, Byron, Browning, Shelley, Emerson, Walt Whitman. Where are their equals among women? And coming down to the modern period, when literature is flooded with feminine figures, is there one who can be placed beside Anatole France or d'Annunzio or Proust or Gorki or even Bernard Shaw (not to mention Ibsen)? The feminine names that might be cited in comparison are obvious enough, but would any of them measure up to these—quite? However, let me mention Katherine Mansfield, Edith Wharton, Edna St. Vincent Millay. And I may add Sheila Kaye-Smith, Willa Cather, Selma Lagerlöf and Marguérite Audou.

I realize, of course, that such comparisons, except in a most sweeping statement, are invidious. A better picture could be obtained by juxtaposing, one to one, writers of similar type and literary form—but this is a task for a volume.

Caruso or deReszke, a Morini or Powell or Parlow to match a Heifetz or Elman or Kreisler; but there is no woman to match a Beethoven or Wagner or Strauss or Mahler or Stravinsky, or Rachmaninoff—a composer-performer.

The situation in drama is almost equally illuminating. Here women have reached the top, have done it so frequently and persistently, in fact, as to challenge men, some think successfully so. But as dramatic writers the few women who tried have never succeeded to rise above moderate excellence. A Rachel or Duse can hold her own as against a Possart or Orlenyev, a Bernhardt looms as high as an Irving, Booth or Salvini; but there is no woman to compare with a Molière or Ostrovski or Rostand or Hauptmann or Chekhov or Kapek.

If now we glance once more at the primitive record the conclusion suggested by an analysis of music and the drama is greatly reënforced. In primitive society woman, whenever opportunity was given her, equaled man in creativeness; in modern society she has uniformly failed in the highest ranges. The results are not incompatible. As indicated before, in early days cultural conditions precluded the exercise of creativeness on the part of the individual except on a minor scale, in modern society major creativeness is possible and has been realized. Woman's creative achievement reaches the top when the top is relatively low; when the top itself rises, she falls behind.

To analyze this fact further is no easy task. We may not assume, as some do, that the difference between major and minor creativeness lies in degrees of rationality. This is certainly erroneous. The true creator is what he is, not because of his rationality but because of what he does with it. The differentia, as I see them, are two: boldness of imagination and tremendous concentration on self. The creator, when he creates, is spiritually alone; he dominates his material by drawing it into the self and he permits his imagination, for once torn off the moorings of tradition and precedent, to indulge in flights of gigantic sweep. Imagination and personality exalted to the nth power—not rationality—are the marks of the highest creativeness.

In the possession of these traits, then, as here understood, woman is somehow restricted. She has them, of course, and exercises them, but not on the very highest level.

We might stop right here, but it is hard to suppress at least a tentative interpretation.

If the personality-imagination complex is where woman fails at the top, then it becomes *a priori* probable that this difference between man and woman constitutes a remote sex characteristic. And if this is so, then it may prove worth our while to look for a corresponding difference on a level more directly connected with sex life. No sooner is this done than a difference does indeed appear, and it meets our expectations, for it lies in the direction of personality or self-concentration as well as of imagination. Woman is never so much "a part of" as when she loves, man never so "whole"; her self dissolves, his crystallizes. Also, woman's love is less imaginative than man's: man is more like what woman's love makes him out to be than woman is like what man's love makes her out to be. Relatively speaking, his love is romantic, hers realistic.

This difference in the diagnostic features of man's love and woman's love confirms our suspicion that the discrepancy in performance, where the personality-imagination complex is involved, constitutes a remote sex characteristic.

We must now turn once more to woman's achievement in the different fields of cultural creativeness, for the variation in the degree of excellence reached by her provides a valuable clue as to where her strength lies. In an ascending series of woman's achievements musical composition is at the bottom of the list, then come sculpture and painting, then literature (with a strange drop in dramatic writing), then instrumental and vocal performance; acting, finally, heads the list.

This order is most illuminating. The relative excellence of woman's achievement is seen to rise with the concreteness of the task and the prominence of the technical and human elements. Creativeness is more abstract in music than in the plastic and graphic arts, more abstract in these than in literature; and in each case woman's relative achievement increases as abstractness decreases. Even the peculiar drop in dramatic writing when compared with other forms of literature is explicable in terms of a more abstract sort of creativeness required by the formal elements of dramatic art. Again, the high position in the list of musical performers and actresses, must in part be ascribed to the importance of the technical element in these arts. The preeminence of the musical performers is probably entirely due to this factor, although the intrusion of the human element (performing for an audience) may also have a share in the result.

In the case of acting the human element is the most important factor, for here there is not only an audience to act to but the human content of the acting itself. The human orientation also accounts for the relatively high position of literature in the list when compared to sculpture and painting and to musical composition. Finally, the creativeness of musical performance and acting—two fields in which woman excels—is concrete when compared to that of literature, the arts and musical composition. Incidentally, a sidelight is thus thrown on the case of science where woman's relative preëminence is found in the concrete and technical domain of the laboratory.

The preceding analysis leads to the conclusion that woman's strength lies in the concrete as contrasted with the abstract, the technical as contrasted with the ideational, the human as contrasted with the universal and detached. This conclusion, it may be of interest to note, harmonizes perfectly with the general consensus of mankind, as expressed in lay opinion and the judgments of literary men.

To summarize: in all fields of cultural activity opened to her, woman has shown creative ability, but since cultural conditions have made major creativeness possible, she has failed, in comparison with man, in the highest ranges of abstract creativeness. On the other hand, woman has shown in her psychic disposition affinities for the concrete, the technical and the human.

Before closing, these findings may be utilized for a prognostication of woman's activities in the immediate and more remote future.

The present tendency toward equalizing the cultural opportunities of man and woman will no doubt persist. Thus the range of woman's cultural contributions will expand and the excellence of her creative achievement will rise, especially in the fields in which she has so far had but little chance to try her hand. It is to be expected, however, that in the highest ranges of abstract creativeness in philosophy, science, art, music, and perhaps literature, she will fail as she has hitherto failed to equal man. Her concrete-mindedness will ever continue to provide a useful counterpoise to the more imaginative and abstract leanings of her male companion. Her technical talents will shine more brilliantly in a world in which the crafts will again occupy the prominent place which was theirs once before. But her unique contributions will come in the range of the human element.

In this respect, woman's principal affinity is calculated to bear its choicest fruits in a world better than the one we live in. When formalism recedes from the field of education, as indeed it has already begun to do, and gives room for more individual and psychologically refined processes, woman's share in education will grow in scope and creativeness. When the family has left behind the agonies of its present readjustments, the reconstruction of a freer and happier family life will largely rest on the shoulders of woman. When prisons will be turned into hospitals and criminals will be treated as patients, woman's sensitiveness, insight and tact will bring her leadership in this field. When a return of leisure and the reduction of economic pressure will permit a revival of the more intimate forms of social intercourse, woman's social talents will find new fields to conquer. When the world of nations will sheathe its sword forever—an event toward the realization of which woman will probably contribute more than man—woman, to whom nothing human is foreign, will at last be free to show the world what she can accomplish as the mother of the family of man.

Dominant Sexes
By M. Vaerting

M. Vaerting,

one of a group of German anthropologists whose lectures and articles have attracted much attention in Europe; is also part author of "The Dominant Sex," recently published in the United States.

DOMINANT SEXES

BY M. VAERTING

CERTAIN peculiarities of physical form are to-day considered typical feminine sex characters. Thus roundness and fullness of figure are generally regarded as characteristic of women; larger size and strength among men are accepted as a sex difference, biologically determined.

But this theory, like the entire doctrine of secondary sex characters, stands upon a doubtful basis. It has grown up out of a comparison of men and women in very unequal situations. The bodies of men and women whose field of work and type of occupation differ widely have been compared. The man attends to the extra-domestic activities, while the woman is chiefly occupied at home. Bachofen writes: "If a man sits at a spinning-wheel a weakening of body and of soul will inevitably follow." Charles de Coster in his "Wedding Journey" makes the significant remark: "Work in the fields had given Liska hips like a robust man's." Certain of the physical differences between men and women may therefore be sociologically determined rather than due to inborn differences.

One may object that the division of labor between the sexes, in which the woman takes the domestic and the man the extra-domestic sphere, is itself determined by inborn sex differences. Even in Socrates's time it was believed that the nature of the sexes fixed their fields of activity. Man was unquestionably intended for matters which must be attended to outside the house, "while the weak and timid woman was by divine order assigned to the inner work of the home." After thorough investigation it appears that this hoary theory, which still persists, is false. The division of labor between man and woman corresponds not to an innate difference but to their power-relation. If man dominates he says that woman's place is the home, and that work outside the home is fit only for men. If woman is dominant then she has the opposite opinion, takes care of business outside the home, and leaves the man to take care of the family and the housekeeping. The ruling sex, whether male or fe-

male, always puts the domestic duties on the subordinate sex and takes to itself work outside the
home. To-day man is dominant, but there have
been many peoples among whom woman was
dominant and the rôle of man and woman was
the reverse of that common to-day. In ancient
Egypt there was a period when women ruled.
Herodotus reports that they unnaturally performed "masculine" activities, carried on commerce in the market-place, while the men stayed
at home, sewed, and attended to domestic difficulties. To Herodotus, who came from a state
where men were dominant, the work of the
Egyptian women naturally seemed "male." In
the Talmud Herodotus's report is confirmed.
The children of Israel, it tells us, were disturbed
because their men were forced to do women's
work and their women men's work. In Sopho-
cles's "Œdipus Kolonos" Œdipus says to his
two daughters: "Ha, how they imitate the Egyptians in the manner and meaning of life. There
the men stay home and sit at the spinning-wheel,
and the women go out to meet the needs of life."
Œdipus also mentions the fact reported also by
Herodotus, that only the daughters, not the sons,

were compelled in Egypt to support their parents. The sons could not fulfill that duty, Sopho-
cles says, because, like the Greek girls, they
stayed at home and had no income from their
labor. Furthermore, they had only a limited
right to own property.

One might cite many other peoples where the
woman was dominant. Among the Kamchadales
the men, in the days of female dominance, were
such complete housewives that they cooked,
sewed, washed, and were never allowed to stay
away from home for more than a day. Similarly
among the Lapps there was a period when the
men did the housework while the women fished
and sailed the sea. Under such circumstances
the men also took care of the children. Strabo
and Humboldt both report of the Vasko-Iberian
races that the women worked in the fields; after
child birth they turned the child over to the man
and themselves resumed their work in the fields.
A similar arrangement prevailed in the days
when women ruled Lybia, which bordered upon
Egypt.

When one sex is dominant there is always a
division of labor.

This differentiation of occupation is one of the chief causes of certain differences in physical form between men and women. It changes the fundamental conditions of development—among others the course of the inner secretions. Where man rules he does the active outside work and is accordingly larger and stronger; where woman rules and does the same "man's work" her body assumes what are to-day regarded as typically male proportions, whereas the man develops what we call feminine characteristics. We have a few definite proofs of this from states dominated by women.

When woman ruled among the Gauls, and worked outside the home, we are told by Strabo that the female was the larger and stronger sex.

Among the Adombies on the Congo women were in power and did all the hard work. According to Ellis they were stronger and better developed than the men. The same was true of the Wateita in East Africa. Fritsch and Hellwald report that the woman is larger than the man among the Bushmen. Female and male pelvises show no differences, but are alike "male" in our sense of the word.

The Spartan women in the days of their rule had a reputation for enormous strength. Aristophanes says that a Spartan woman could strangle an ox bare-handed. The Egyptian women at the height of their power were called by their neighbors the "lionesses of the Nile," and they seemed to like the name. When Heracles visited the Lybians, whose state bordered on Egypt and of whose rule by women we have many witnesses, he had to work, like the other men of the country, with the distaff. His wife Omphale, however, wandered about clad in a lionskin and armed with a club, and won respect for her strength.

A very striking report comes from near New Guinea, where the woman was stronger than the man. There it was a common sight to see a woman spanking her husband with a paddle. Through the brute force of superior strength she oppressed the man just as men oppress women where the woman is weaker.

Thus through legend and the records of travelers we have clear testimony that man is not larger and stronger than woman because of innate differences, as is generally supposed, but that physical superiority is a characteristic of the dominant sex, regardless whether that be male or female.

Similarly those secondary physical characteristics which are to-day regarded as female are found among males when they occupy the subordinate position in which woman lives to-day. Woman is inclined to-day to full, rounded curves and even to stoutness. Among the Celts the woman dominated, and according to Strabo the men of that people were inclined to be fat and heavy-paunched. The same was true of the Kamchadales in the days of woman rule. The men were strikingly voluptuous and well rounded. The male Eskimos too were inclined to fatness in the days when they did the housekeeping. The more subordinate the fatter.

In this connection the Oriental women are typical; their exuberance of figure is as well known as their absolute subordination and their confinement to the home. They may be contrasted with the fat and subordinate male Kamchadales, whose wives were slim and firm breasted into old age.

Equal rights do away with this division of

labor. There are no longer male and female jobs; not sex but inclination and fitness now begin to determine the individual's occupation. In late Egypt, when the domination of woman was merging into a period of equal rights, there are many indications that both sexes did the same work without any differentiation of occupation. In the marriage contract in the time of Darius, the woman—who then made the contract alone— says, "All, which you and I may together earn. . . ." Victor Marx has studied the position of woman in Babylon in the period 604-485 B.C., and finds a similar situation. In an inheritance case of that period a woman recites that "I and my husband carried on business with my dowry and together bought a piece of land." Such common businesses by man and woman are frequently mentioned. Under such circumstances it was natural that neither man nor woman bound themselves at marriage to live in the same house, for both went to work outside the home.

To-day, when we are passing from male domination to equal rights it is natural that the woman should be seeking more and more to get out of the home. The greater her power the more she seeks to level the lines between male and female work. This effort is strongest in the subordinate sex—in this case the feminine—because it seeks naturally to better its position. In this transition period, therefore, women are pressing into male pursuits much faster than men into domestic occupations. Yet even in Germany a beginning has been made. For women the male professions seem higher and better, because they have hitherto belonged to the dominant sex, while for the men feminine occupations seem to have about them something degrading; but the more women approach equality the less odium attaches to what has been their sphere, and the more men tend to enter it.

The same phenomenon may be observed in periods of transition from female to male domination. Among the Batta, for instance, both sexes worked in the fields, but the man alone cared for the children. This was obviously a step toward equal rights. The men already shared the extra-domestic occupations of the women, but the women still refused to share the work of the hitherto subordinate men.

When equal rights put an end to the differentiation of occupation the physical differences between men and women also disappear. We are to-day still far enough away from equality of the sexes, but there have been people where equal rights prevailed, and among such people the physical form of the two sexes was so like that they could hardly be distinguished. In Tacitus's day, when equality was probably general among the Germans, men and women are reported to have had exactly the same weight and strength. Albert Friedenthal says of the Cingalese that a stranger could not distinguish the sexes. Men and women were so alike among the Botocudos that one had to count their tresses to tell them apart. Lallemant found among this people "a swarm of men-women and women-men, not a single man or a single woman in the whole tribe." This good man came from a state where men dominated and did not suspect that when the power-relation of the sexes changed their physical appearance changed too. If a Botocudo had come to Europe in those days he would presumably have judged by his own standards and noted with equal horror the outer differences of European men and women.

Every age holds its own standards absolute. The domination of one sex depends upon the artificial development of as many and as striking bodily differences as possible, and therefore approves them and insists upon emphasizing them. Equal rights tend to develop the natural similarity of the sexes and considering that the norm, regards it as ideal.

There is ample opportunity to observe to-day that equality of the sexes coincides with a tendency slowly to do away with artificial physical differences. The disappearance of the so-called feminine figure was so striking in America, where the sexes are more nearly equal than in Europe, that Sargent and Alexander prophesied in 1910 that soon men and women could hardly be distinguished from one another. A comparison with pictures of thirty or forty years ago makes it plain that even in Europe male and female figures are coming closer to each other. The narrow waists and full bosoms of the women and the full beards of the men have disappeared. And, as a result of our investigation, we may prophesy that the coming equality will still more completely iron out those differences which hitherto have been regarded as genuine secondary sex characters.

Whenever one sex is dominant there is a tendency to differentiate male and female costume. The more completely one sex dominates the greater will be the differences in clothes, and as the sexes become equal the differences disappear. When the two sexes are really equal they will wear the same clothing.

The clothing of the dominant sex usually tends to be uniform and tasteless, that of the subordinate to be varied and richly ornamented. Today man is still dominant, and his clothes are monotonous, dull, and less subject to shifts of fashion. Especially in formal dress he wears a sort of uniform. All men, of whatever age or position, wear dress clothes of the same cut and color. A grandfather wears a dinner coat exactly like that of his eighteen-year-old grandson. This seems natural, but the situation is reversed with the subordinate sex, most completely when the subordination is most complete. Only twenty or thirty years ago it was a crime in Germany for a mother to dress as "youthfully" as her unmarried daughter. A grandmother who dared to dress like her eighteen-year-old granddaughter would have been laughed to scorn. As woman's power has grown, this has changed. Custom no longer requires a grandmother to emphasize her age by her clothes.

Where woman dominates she tends to wear darker and plainer clothing and the man dresses himself more richly and variously. Erman writes of the old Egyptians:

> While according to our conceptions it befits the woman to love finery and ornament, the Egyptians of the old Empire seem to have had an opposite opinion. Beside the elaborate costumes of the men the women's clothing seems very monotonous, for, from the fourth to the eighteenth dynasty, all, from the king's daughter to the peasant woman, wore the same garb—a simple garment without folds.

Herodotus, indeed, reported that Egyptian men had two suits, women only one. Erman naturally cannot explain the simplicity of the women's clothes and the eagerness of the men for color and ornament, because it contradicted current theories of the character of the two sexes. To-day the view is current which Runge expressed when he said that "Women's desire to please and love of ornament is dependent upon her sex life." This view, though still common, is fundamentally false. The inclination to bright and ornamental clothing is dependent not upon sex but upon the power-relation of the sexes. The subordinate sex, whether male or female, seeks ornament. Strabo tells of the love of finery and cult of the body among Lybian men. They curled their hair, even their beards, wore gold ornaments, diligently brushed their teeth and polished their finger-nails. "They arrange their hair so tenderly," he writes, "that when walking they never touch one another, in order not to disturb it." It is usual in states where women are dominant for the men to wear long hair and pay particular attention to their barbering. The men of Tana, in the Hebrides, wore their hair 18 to 20 inches long, divided into six or seven hundred tiny locks, in the days when women ruled. Among the Latuka the men wore their hair so elaborately that it took ten years to arrange it. The Konds also wore very long hair, elaborately arranged.

The stronger tendency of the subordinate sex to ornamentation apparently is closely related to the division of labor. The subordinate sex, working at home, has more leisure and opportunity for ornament than the dominant. Furthermore, leisure stimulates the erotic feelings. Since the partner does not share the leisure the lonely erotic often seeks a way out in self-ornamentation. At the same time the ornament is intended for the partner, for the stimulated eroticism increases the desire to please the other sex.

When the sexes are equal the clothes of the two sexes tend to be alike. We have noted that the Cingalese were physically similar; their clothes were exactly the same. The only difference was that the men wore a mother-of-pearl comb in the hair, the women none. Among the Lepka the sexes can be distinguished only by the fact that the men wear their hair in two braids, the women in one. Tacitus reports that the old Germans wore the same clothes and wore their hair alike.

We can observe the tendency to similarity of costume in this transition period. Many such attempts fail the first time, but finally succeed. More than a decade ago Paris attempted to establish a fashion of knickerbockers and bobbed hair. The attempt failed, but to-day the bobbed head has invaded every civilized country, almost in direct proportion to the degree in which women have acquired equal rights. It is reported from England that English women can already go to their work in trousers, heavy shoes, and short hair without exciting attention. The reader may judge of the accuracy of these reports. In Germany the police forbid one sex to wear the clothes of the other, but during the war when German women had to enter male trades they usually wore men's clothing.

Among men too the tendency to similarity is evident. Thirty years ago the beard was a generally accepted sign of manhood; it has fallen out of fashion. In the Youth Movement there is a tendency to leave the shirt open at the neck and to adopt a hair-cut like a bobbed girl's. A note in Jean Paul's "Levana," which appeared in 1806, is interesting. He writes: "A few years ago it was fashionable in Russia for the men to fill out their clothing with high false bosoms." That was in the days following the French Revolution, when a short wave of freedom, even for women, swept across the earth. It showed also in the women's fashion which Jean Paul mentions:

A fortunate accident for daughters is the Grecian costume of the present Gymnosophists (naked female runners), which, it is true, injures the mothers but hardens the daughters; for as age and custom should avoid every fresh cold so youth exercises itself on it as on every hardship until it can bear greater. . . . So, likewise, the present naked manner of dressing is a cold bath into which the daughters are dipped, who are exhilarated by it.

Modern Love and Modern Fiction
By J. W. Krutch

Joseph Wood Krutch

has been Professor of English at the Brooklyn Polytechnic Institute, and is now dramatic editor and regular critic of fiction of The Nation.

MODERN LOVE AND MODERN FICTION

BY J. W. KRUTCH

SEEING upon the jacket of a recent book the legend "Solves the Sex Problem," my first reaction was a fervent hope that it did nothing of the sort, for I had no desire that fiction should be rendered supererogatory or, what is the same thing, that life should be made a less difficult art. Problems of housing, wages, taxation, militarism, and the like may be solved, temporarily at least, but what a contemporary writer has called "the irony of being two" is a sufficient guaranty of one never-to-be-resolved complexity. Until each individual of the human species becomes a complete biological entity, until, that is to say, hermaphrodism is universal, there can be no fear lest we should cease to live dangerously.

Were I speaking of happiness I should be compelled to argue that the attitude of society and the individual toward sex is the most important thing in the world, but speaking as I am of life as material for art I must maintain, on the contrary, that it is much less important. As long as they have an attitude and as long as that attitude remains, as it has always remained, an inadequate one, those unresolved discords which make living and reading interesting will continue to arise. As a critic I "view with alarm" nothing except the possibility that the problem should be solved to everybody's satisfaction, but that calamity does not seem at all likely to occur since I have never heard of a saint in the desert or a debauché in a brothel who was not sufficiently maladjusted to be a fruitful subject for fiction.

After all, the things we do are both more significant and less changing than our attitude toward our acts. We burn men at the stake to light a Roman garden, to save the world from the horror of heresy, or to protect the sanctity of female virtue and assure the supremacy of the white race, but we burn them always; we fight because arms are glorious, because the service of God demands the rescue of His holy sepulcher from the infidel, or because we must make the world safe for peace, but always we fight; and the most important thing is the insistent lust of cruelty or the impulse to fight rather than the rationalization of these motives. So, too, with love. Paphnutius is harried out of apathy into a state in which he sees visions because of the temptations of the devil, Milton because God gave Eve to Adam as a comforter, Shelley because woman is the symbol of the unutterable, and Shaw (presumably) because only by the process of reproduction can the Life Force perform its perfectionist experiments; but the resultant impulses are not so very different. Mr. F. W. Myers once referred to the procreation of children in these lines:

> Lo! When a man magnanimous and tender,
> Lo! When a woman desperate and true,
> Make the inevitable sweet surrender,
> Show one another what the Lord can do, . . .

but I doubt if the states of mind which called forth these lines and, say, Swinburne's Dolores were as different as the verses would suggest or as the authors imagined. Without going so far as to say that the two poems are of equal literary

merit, one can at least say that they are almost
equally interesting and delightful to the ob-
server of life or art and that as long as the
mystical, the ascetic, the sentimental, and the
biological attitudes toward love continue to exist side by side or to follow one another in suc-
ceeding epochs, the critic will not find literature either dull or monotonous.

If at the end of a period of twenty-five years
during which fiction has frankly concerned itself
to an unusual degree with sex the problem seems
more complicated than ever before, there is no
cause for surprise. Even the specious pretense
that a solution has been found can only be maintained when, as during the Victorian era, the
mass of men agree to assume that no difficulties
exist which are not solvable by that rule of
thumb known as the social and moral code, and
insist that sexual battles shall be fought out behind closed doors in life and between the chapters in books. By dragging them out into public
view we have been able, no doubt, to palliate
some of the commoner tragedies of stupidity.
But chiefly we have been upon a voyage of discovery, and it ought to be evident now, if it has

never been evident before, that we cannot possibly solve the problem because its most important aspects are not social but human. They have their roots in man's ironic predicament between gorilla and angel, a predicament perfectly typified by the fact that as he grows critical he realizes that love is at once sublime and obscene and that only by walking a spiritual tight-rope above the abysses can he be said to live at all in any true sense. The very fact that the social aspects can to a certain extent be worked out makes them less interesting and explains the fact that those novels intended to prove, for example, that the mother of an illegitimate child may still be within the human pale have come to seem so unutterably dull. No doubt they "did good," but like all forms of useful literature their life was short. By far the most interesting contemporary writers who deal chiefly with sex are largely concerned with the individual problem.

Thanks partially to modern fiction we have attained a certain measure of freedom. But freedom, as everybody who understands either the meaning of the word or the value of the thing knows, raises problems instead of settling them. It is true that our attitude has changed. There is hardly a serious contemporary novel which does not take for granted things which would have outraged even liberal thinkers of the past century, and the changes have been mostly in the direction of clarification. It would be impossible for any one to-day to fail to see, as George Eliot failed to see, that the natural working of the "inevitable moral law" which punished Hetty Sorrel was neither inevitable nor natural. The things which happened to her came entirely from society and not at all from nature, so that the story which the author meant to be a tragedy of the ineluctable becomes merely a description of human stupidity. So, too, we are clearer on other things; we are not quite so hopelessly at sea as we once were when it comes to distinguishing between frigidity and chastity or purity and prudishness. But these things mean only that more choices are open to us, that we have come to see that sexual conduct cannot be guided or judged by a few outwardly applied standards, and that, accordingly, the conduct of life has been made more thrillingly difficult.

Most sex novels of the past have been concerned chiefly with what might be called the right to love. They have combated an extremely old idea which Christianity found congenial and embodied in the conception of love as a part of the curse pronounced upon man at the Fall, and hence at best a necessary evil. They have been compelled solemnly to assure us that the early Christian Fathers were wrong in assuming that the human race would have been better off if it had been able to propagate itself by means of some harmless system of vegetation, and they have had to fly in the face of all laws and social customs which are seen, if examined closely, to rest upon the assumption that desire is merely a dangerous nuisance, fatal to efficiency and order, and hence to be regimented at any cost. It is now pretty generally admitted among the educated class that love is legitimate, even that it has anæsthetic as well as a utilitarian function. We have got back to the point which Ovid had reached some two thousand years ago of realizing that there is an art of love. During the next quarter of a century fiction will be concerned, I think, more with the failure or success of individuals to attain this art than with the exposition of theses which most accept.

No doubt some of the more naïvely enthusiastic crusaders really believed that as soon as man was freed from the more grossly stupid restrictions from without and from the artificially cultivated inhibitions within, love would become simple and idyllic, but one needs look only at the books of D. H. Lawrence or Aldous Huxley to be relieved of this stupid delusion. The characters of both of these authors have long ago ceased to care what law or society thinks and they are surely untroubled by traditional asceticism, but their problems are not less acute. Indeed it is just because these novelists are so completely concerned with love as a personal matter that they are the freshest of those contemporary writers with whom sex is the dominant interest. Each is concerned with something fundamental—the one with the problem of the adjustment of personalities and the other with the evaluation of sexual love.

If by "immoral" is meant "tending to excite lubricity," then nothing could be more absurd than the opinion, apparently held by some, that the books of these men are immoral. They are so completely unable to lose themselves carelessly in passion and so insistent upon the need of adjusting it somehow to the other interests of life that they strike one as more like saints than like gallants, and their books are far more chilling than inflammatory. Huxley and Joyce try to laugh sex away, but their scorn of the flesh suggests Erasmus more than Rabelais, and, as for Lawrence, his novels constitute so solemn a warning that one imagines him as thoroughly bored with the exigencies of passion and more likely to make his disciples celibates than debauchés.

In Lawrence's morbidly sensitive and exaggeratedly individualistic characters one sees as through a magnifying-glass the thousand impingements of personality upon personality which make love more and more difficult as it becomes more intimate and personal. His people, like Schopenhauer's porcupines, are continually coming together for warmth only to find themselves pricked by one another's quills and to part snarling, so that his perpetual prayer is a "Lord deliver us from this need which can be neither stilled nor satisfied." And abnormal though he is, his abnormality is one of degree only, for when sexual love is developed beyond the impulse of the animal and desires the contact of spirit as well as body that contact is bound to be both incomplete and painful.

Nor is the even more fundamental problem with which Aldous Huxley is concerned likely ever to receive a permanent or a general solution. He is in search of love, but he can find only ridiculous and obscene biological facts, for love, like God and the other most important human possessions, does not exist. It is an illusion created by the effort of the imagination to transform the unsatisfactory materials which life has furnished it into something acceptable to the soul; but being an illusion, it is unstable and perpetually tending, if not created anew, to dissolve into its elements. The racial need for the continuation of the species and the individual need for the satisfaction of a physiological impulse exist, but they are hard, unsatisfying realities, and the struggle of mankind is to create some fiction which will as far as possible include and at the same time transcend them.

And nothing derogatory is, of course, meant by the word "fiction." All that distinguishes man from nature is such a fiction, and it is by his insistent belief in these imaginary things that civilization has been created. All of Mr. Huxley's books are confessions, first cynically triumphant and then despairing, of his inability to be poet or mystic or ironist enough to achieve this transcendence and find in his animal heritage a satisfaction for his spiritual needs. Like everyone else, he is compelled to love, and love implies a certain amount of idealization. How, he asks in effect, is he to poetize this ridiculous function, which he shares with the beasts, and concerning which science is constantly presenting us with an increasing amount of disillusioning knowledge? Exercising the most perverse ingenuity in confronting romance with biology and in establishing the identity (in the realm of fact) of love and lust, he has continually tracked the trail of the beast into the holy of holies—but only because it hurt him so much to find it there. The obscenities in which he seems to revel are defiances of the inner idealist who has dared to assimilate the loathsome trivialities of sex into

something capable of satisfying spiritual desires.
When he sings one of his philosopher's songs or
when, in "Antic Hay," he describes some particularly revolting orgy there is nothing new in
the psychological state which provokes his obscenity. His attitude is a result of failure to
reconcile physical fact with spiritual feeling.
He is not far from Huysmans, who ended "A
Rebours" with the words: "For the man who
has written such a book there are only two alter-
natives—a pistol or the foot of the cross." Only
of course Huysmans was wrong. Anatole
France and James Branch Cabell are not less
sophisticated, but through the perfection of
sophistication they have achieved a peaceful
irony in which they can worship a non-existent
God and believe again in the illusions they
create. Huxley, too sophisticated for simple
faith and too downright for ironic worship, is
lost.

When the conception of love is, as it has
tended to be in modern times, legalistic, these
problems are submerged. As long as marriage
is a matter of contract, the importance of the
inward harmony of personalities is of the slight-

est, for children may be begotten and reared whether the parents love or hate. As long as passion is generally conceded to be but a shameful concession to unregenerate humanity, the average man is not likely to be concerned if he finds that the ideal of the poets is not realized in his own nuptial couch. But when love is free and unashamed then it is made ten times more difficult, for lives are recognized as frank failures which once would have seemed useful and satisfactory. Fiction, too, becomes, not more interesting, but more important. It ceases completely to be what it always tends to be when opinion is fixed, namely, a mere illustration of the working out of social or moral "laws"; it becomes frankly the record of individual souls in search of a successful way of life. It records, no doubt, more failures than successes, but it furnishes the best and perhaps only really important material for the study of that art of life which grows ever more complicated as we demand that it be more complete and beautiful.

Can Men and Women Be Friends?
By Floyd Dell

Floyd Dell

was born at Barry, Illinois, June 28th, 1887. Is the author of several novels and collections of essays including "Janet March," a story of a young woman and her adjustment to modern standards. His latest book is "Looking at Life." Other books are "Women as World Builders," 1913; "Were You Ever a Child?" 1919; "Moon Calf," 1920; "The Briary Bush," 1921.

CAN MEN AND WOMEN BE FRIENDS?

BY FLOYD DELL

FRIENDSHIP between men and women is rather a new thing in the history of the world. Friendship depends upon equality and choice, and there has been very little of either in the relations of the sexes, up to the present. A woman does not choose her male relatives, nor is she according to archaic family laws their equal; motives other than personal choice might lead her to become a man's wife; wholly impersonal reasons might place her in the relationship of kept mistress. Only in her rôle of paramour was there any implication of free choice; and even here there was no full equality, not even of danger. None of these customary relationships of the past can be said to have fostered friendship between men and women. Doubtless it did exist, but under difficulties.

Family bonds, however, are being more and more relaxed, women are no longer the wards of

their male relatives, and friendship with a father
or brother is more than ever possible. Further,
the free personal choice which marked only the
romantic amours of the age of chivalry is now
popularly regarded in America as essential to
any decent marriage, while the possibility of
divorce tends to make free choice something be-
sides a mere youthful illusion. More than ever
before, husbands and wives are friends.

At the same time the intensity of friendships
between people of the same sex appears to be
diminishing. This intensity, in its classic instances, as in Greece, we now regard as an artificial product, the result of the segregation of the
sexes and the low social position of women. As
women become free and equal with men such
romantic intensity of emotion finds a more biologically appropriate expression. Friendships
between people of the same sex must to-day compete on the one hand with romantic love and on
the other with the more fascinating though often
less enduring friendships which can now be enjoyed between men and women. Neglect of
these latter opportunities is coming to be re-

garded as a kind of spiritual cowardice, or at least as a failure in enterprise.

The influences of the machine age, so destructive to fixed authoritarian relationships, appear to foster the growth of friendship between the sexes; so much so that we may expect it to become, in its further developments, a characteristic social feature of the age that lies immediately before us.

Friendship will become a more and more important aspect of marriage itself; but, except in the effects of its wider spread, this will hardly be a new thing—we have friendships between husbands and wives now. Nor will extra-marital friendships between men and women be precisely a new thing. What will be new, furnishing us with an interesting theme for sociological speculation, are the conventions which will gradually come into existence to give social protection and dignity to extra-marital friendships.

Conventions are, doubtless, always rather ridiculous, inevitably a shackle upon the free motions of the soul, being imposed by fear. But it will be remembered that we, in America, with

a vast amount of freedom of intersexual association, have thus far only begun to dispense with
the locks and bars and whippings and chaperons
which were the appurtenances of a physical segregation of the sexes; the vast paraphernalia of
psychic segregation, including sexual taboos
which hark back to the primeval darkness, are
with us still. Our minds are habituated to unreasonable fears in all matters concerning the
relations of the sexes. For a long time, extra-
marital friendships of men and women may be
expected to be hedged about with elaborate and
specific permissions, for the sake of keeping
them under social control. Yet these conventions may be very convenient; and however irk-
some they may seem to the free spirits of a future
day, they may still be such as would appear to
us generously libertarian.

To-day, in the absence of such conventions, it
does not suffice that a man and woman, too well
married to be afraid of extra-marital friendships, grant them to each other by private treaty;
relatives, friends, and neighbors do not fail to be
duly alarmed. Extra-marital friendship exists

in an atmosphere of social suspicion which a few conventions would go far to alleviate.

As an example in a different field, the convention with regard to dancing may be adduced. If dancing were not a general custom, if it were the enlightened practice of an advanced few, how peculiar and suspicious would seem the desire of Mr. X and Mrs. Y to embrace each other to music; and how scandalized the neighbors would be to hear that they *did!* No one would rest until the pair had been driven into an elopement.

We build huge palaces for the kind of happy communion which dancing furnishes; we tend more and more to behave like civilized beings about the impulses which are thus given scope. We are less socially hospitable to the impulses of friendship between men and women.

In friendship there are many moods; but the universal rite of friendship is *talk*. Talk needs no palaces for its encouragement; it is not an expensive affair; it would seem to be well within the reach of all. Yet it isn't. For the talk of friendship requires privacy—though the privacy of a table for two in a crowded and noisy restaurant will suffice; and it requires time. Such talk does not readily adjust itself to the limitations of the dinner hour. It is a flower slow in unfolding; and it seems to come to its most perfect bloom only after midnight. But, unfortunately, not every restaurant keeps open all night. It is satisfied with two comfortable chairs; a table to lean elbows on is good, too; in winter an open fire, where friendly eyes may stare dreamily into the glowing coals—that is very good; hot or cold drinks according to the season, and a cigarette—these are almost the height of friendship's luxury. These seem not too much to ask. Yet the desire for privacy and uncounted hours of time together is, when considered from that point of view, scandalous in its implications; quite as much so as the desire of Mr. X and Mrs. Y to embrace each other to music. However, Mr. X and Mrs. Y do, under the ægis of a convention, indulge their desire and embrace each other to their heart's content with the full approval of civilized society; and it seems as though another convention might grow up, under the protection of which Mr. X and Mrs. Y might sit up and talk all night without its seeming queer of them.

Queer, at the least, it does seem nowadays, except under the conventions of courtship; friends who happen to be married to each other can of course talk comfortably in bed. These bare facts are sufficient to explain why so many men and women who really want to be friends and sit up all night occasionally and talk find it easy to believe that they are in love with each other. They find it all the easier to believe this, because friendship between the sexes is usually spiced with some degree of sexual attraction. But a degree of sexual attraction which might have kept a friendship forever sweet may prove unequal to the requirements of a more serious and intimate relationship. Disillusionment is the penalty, at the very least. Society could well afford to grant more freedom to friendship between men and women, and save the expense of a large number of broken hearts.

It is worth while to wonder if a good deal of "romance" is not, after all, friendship mistaking itself for something else; or rather, finding its only opportunity for expression in that mistake.

Among civilized people, after the romance has ended, the friendship remains. It may perhaps have been worth while to imagine oneself in love, in order to enjoy a friendship; but it seems rather a wasteful proceeding.

Yet those who, taking a merely economical view of the situation, attempt to enjoy such friendships without becoming involved or involving others in such waste, may with some embarrassment discover—what Mrs. Grundy could have told them all along—that friendship and sexual romance may sometimes be difficult to relegate to previously determined boundaries. Friendship between the sexes may, if only for a moment, seem to demand the same tokens of sincerity as romantic love. Does not this fact threaten the traditional, jealously-guarded dignity of marriage?

Perhaps it does. At present, in any conflict of claims between a marriage and a friendship, there is "nothing to arbitrate"; marriage has all the rights, friendship none. If the rights of friendship are to be at all considered and protected, marriage may have to yield something. It may not be good manners for husbands and wives to be jealous of the quite possible momentary exuberances of each other's friendships; it may be that such incidents will be regarded as being within the discretion of the persons immediately concerned, and not quite proper subjects for inquiry, speculation, or comment by anybody else.

And this might have an effect unsuspected by those whom such a prospect of liberty would most alarm to-day. When a moment's rashness does not necessarily imply red ruin and the breaking up of homes, when sex is freed to a degree from the sense of overwhelming social consequences, it may well become a matter of more profound personal consequence; and with nothing to fear except the spoiling of their friendship, men and women in an ardent friendship may yet prefer talk to kisses.

"But what if they don't?" A complete answer to that question, from the Utopian point of view, would take us far afield from the subject of friendship; yet some further answer may seem to be required, if only by way of confessing to Mrs. Grundy that the problem is not so simple as it may seem. Well, then, out of many possibilities which the future holds, I offer this one for what it may be worth. Such friendships, let us agree, tend to merge insensibly into romantic sexual love. But if marriage may be conceived as yielding some of its traditional rights, extra-marital romance may well be called upon for similar concessions. The first thing that extra-marital romance might be asked to surrender would be its intolerable and fatuous airs of *holiness*. Yes, "holiness" is the word—a holiness all the more asserted by such extra-marital lovers because their relations are likely to be taken disrespectfully by a stupid world. Oh, unquestionably, if you ask them, never was any legal and conventional love so high and holy as this romantic passion of theirs! Its transcendental holiness calls for sacrifices. So they sacrifice themselves—and, incidentally, others—to it. Anything less, they feel, would be cowardly. They must not palter with these sacred emotions —not even by the exercise of their dormant sense of humor!—So it is to-day: but perhaps in a future where extra-marital romance is made room for with a tender and humorous courtesy, it may give up these preposterous and solemn

airs, and actually learn to smile at its illusions—
illusions which will still give the zest of ultimate
danger to relationships of merely happy and
light-hearted play. Thus life will continue to be
interesting.

As for the talk of friendship, my Utopian
speculations uncover for me no respect in which
the thing itself can be improved upon. The circumstances can be made happier, the attitude of
society can foster it; but the talk of friendship
has already reached a splendid perfection beyond
which my imagination is unable to soar. At its
best it has, despite its personal aspect, an impersonal beauty; it is a poignant fulfillment of
those profound impulses which we call curiosity
and candor; it serves human needs as deep as
those which poetry and music serve, and is in
some sense an art like them. The art exists, and
it remains only for the future to give it an adequate hospitality.

Love and Marriage
By Ludwig Lewisohn

Ludwig Lewisohn

author of "Up Stream," "Don Juan" and other books and contributing editor of The Nation, *is now studying conditions in Eastern Europe and Palestine. Was born May 30th, 1882, in Berlin—came to America in 1890—B. A. and M. A. College of Charleston, S. C., 1901—M. A. Columbia, 1903—Editorial staff, Doubleday, Page & Co., 1910-1911. Instructor in German, University of Wisconsin, and Literature at Ohio State University. Dramatic Editor,* Nation, *1919. Author of "The Broken Snare," 1908;—"A Night in Alexandria," 1909; "German Style—an Introduction to the Study of German Prose,"—1910; "The Modern Drama," 1915; "The Spirit of Modern German Literature," 1916; "The Poets of Modern France," 1918; Editor with W. P. Trent of "Letters of an American Farmer," 1909; "A Book of Modern Criticism," 1909. Translator—Feuchlersleben's "Health & Suggestion," 1910; Sudermann's "Judean City," 1911; Halbe's "Youth," Hirschfeld's "The Mothers," 1916; Latzko's "The Judgment of Peace," 1919; Wassermann's "World's Illusion." Editor and chief translator of Gerhardt Hauptmann's Dramatic Works, 1916, 1917; Contributing Editor, Warner's Library of World's Best Literature. His latest book is "The Creative Life," 1924.*

LOVE AND MARRIAGE

BY LUDWIG LEWISOHN

UTOPIA is the loveliest of all countries; it is also the farthest away. One may make magnificent generalizations concerning the future of the relations of the sexes; one may set down truths that are theoretically unanswerable. Only one will change nothing, help not a single soul. Let me cling to a few humble facts. . . .

So far as any one can see the habit of one man living with one woman will persist. The young will hear of nothing else, since they are under the sway of romantic passion which is, subjectively, exclusive and final; those who are older will hear of nothing else because experience has shown this method of life capable of securing the healthiest freedom from preoccupation with sex and the maximum amount of ordered activity. To be a rake or even a fastidious "varietist" is the costliest of occupations. Rational monogamy is in no danger. The trouble lies elsewhere; it

197

lies in the fact that current notions of monogamy are, I use the word advisedly, insane.

Local bill-board advertisements of moving pictures have recently shown a ball-room in which an irate gentleman in evening-dress grasped the shoulder of another gentleman who looked crushed and crest-fallen. With an inimitable gesture of moral indignation the first gentleman pointed to a quivering female on the other side of the room. The caption of this stirring lithograph was "His Forgotten Wife." The exquisite absurdity of this picture is clear. It is significant of the way in which we are all brow-beaten by the sodden nonsense of the tribe that it took me some minutes of reflection to come upon the unreason of the thing. If the crushed looking gentleman had forgotten the lady, she was not, of course, his wife and could never have truly been. If we are dealing with a euphemism and are to understand that he wanted to forget her, she may once have been his wife, but had, quite obviously, ceased to be.

In this moving picture there is illustrated what I call the insane view of monogamic marriage, namely, that it is put on like a shirt or a coat and must be kept on however ill-fitting, comfortless, unclean, or dangerous, and that in this mere keeping on there is virtue. There is the further implication that marriage has nothing to do with good behavior, which is rewarded even in penitentiaries, or with ill; that it is, indeed, an abstract kind of fate, a magical or infernal machine, a metaphysical trap. Once you are caught in it, you must stay caught. To wriggle is sin.

Do I seem to be discussing the matter on too low a plane? I wish I were. The truth is that cultivated and liberal people have not yet freed their minds from the concepts with which that amusing picture deals. It is in action, not in fireside talk that these things are tested. And it is true that even such people will pay an uninhibited respect to a depraved character, cruel, treacherous, stupid, who practices that moving-picture theory of marriage which, in ways no less real for being subtle and but half-conscious, they will be tempted to withhold from a person of the utmost spiritual grace and charm who practices that kind of marriage of which, theoretically and outspokenly, they so eloquently approve.

This very tentative argument, then, is not directed against marriage. I am not even ready to plead—that would be Utopian—that the relations of the sexes be withdrawn from social control. Our first step, at least in America, must be an attempt to sanitate marriage. This can be done—if it can be done at all—by relating marriage and its practice to certain notions of good and decency and honor that already have a tenure, however feeble, upon the public consciousness. Marriage, in brief, should be held to be created by love and sustained by love. I shall, of course, be accused of meaning passion. I mean that precise blending of passion and spiritual harmony and solid friendship without which, as even those who will not admit it know, the close association of a man and a woman is as disgusting as it is degrading. And marriage should be dependent, though this matter is included in the first, on good behavior. I will not keep a man or a woman as my friend whom I discover to be a liar, slanderer, thief. Much less ought one to keep such a person as husband or wife. Who is to judge, it will be asked? No objective judgment is needed. A subjective conviction of this sort suffices to reduce the union in question to dust and ashes.

Here is the one practical point; here the one possibility of hope. To frame a rational theory of the relations of men and women is easy and agreeable. The very fashioners of such theories, being human, will be brought, under the discomforts of social pressure, to *seem* to assent to all that their minds most passionately deny. A man or a woman of the highest philosophic insight will struggle through the ignominy of the divorce courts not so much in order to dissolve a meaningless legal bond as to save some one whom he or she loves and reveres from the criticism of the vulgar. For we live in a vulgar world. There is no safe and ultimate escape; its vulgarity in precisely these matters will often affront us where we least expected it. To mitigate that vulgarity must be our first task.

I do not know whether it can be done at all. But if so, then it must be done by making an unhappy union disgraceful. People who are always bickering with each other, who are obviously unhappy in each other's presence, who always hold opinions acridly opposed, who are always trying either subtly or obviously to escape from each other—such couples must fall under social disapproval. And this disapproval must apply even though one of the two prefers possessiveness to either happiness or decency.or self-respect. Similarly those who are deliberately unfaithful should be disgraced—not for the act of unfaith but for the hypocrisy of remaining in a union which that very act, which the temptation to that very act, shows to have lost its purpose and its meaning.

This sort of social control is not my ideal. Love is like religion, a matter for the individual soul. To change partners in love is very much like changing one's opinion on some deep and vital matter. The spirit must bear its own inherent witness. But I promised myself not to be Utopian. And may it not conceivably be brought home to a few people to begin with that the men who laugh so spontaneously when the song-and-dance man sings "My wife's gone to the country, hurray, hurray!" are leading immoral lives and reducing their partners to the rôle of disagreeable prostitutes and unsatisfactory servants?

I am not prepared to stress the point unendurably. True marriage, the true and lovely union of a man and a woman, body and spirit, is rare. But to-day it is not even an ideal, not even something admired and striven for. Love in itself is rare and married love is perhaps as rare as beauty or genius. Happiness, too, is rare, happiness in any relation. But even as a man or a woman has made an obvious and shattering mistake if his or her chosen work does not produce a reasonable minimum of lasting inner satisfaction, so may marriage also be tested by a reasonable minimum of lasting—let us say, preference and blessedness. To fall below that minimum is to cheat both the self and society, both the present and posterity, to sacrifice honor to a fetish and vitality to decay.

Communist Puritans
By Louis Fischer

Louis Fischer

is Moscow correspondent of the New York Nation

COMMUNIST PURITANS

BY LOUIS FISCHER

THE Soviet state is omnipotent and omnipresent. Bukharin, the arch-theorist, contends that this is a transitional phase in the development of Communism toward perfection. The Bolsheviks' professed aim is the *reductio ad administratum* of the functions of the state; they would make government the traffic cop of the nation but not the all-pervading busybody and touch-everybody-everywhere which it is now in Russia. The transitional period, however, may last long. In default of a world revolution it may project itself beyond the present generation and even beyond the next. And in the meantime it is good Communist doctrine to maintain an Argus-eyed, Herculanean-clubbed state. The Soviet Government is alike an administrator, politician, statesman, merchant, manufacturer, banker, shipbuilder, newspaper publisher, school-teacher, and preacher.

Such a state is the highest expression of the anti-individualism of socialist philosophy. The single *simian erectus* is nothing; it is the class, the nation which counts.

The citizen lives for the state. Mind and muscle must ever be at its service. A Communist who is a loose liver is an anomaly. There is virtue even in a grain of asceticism and in "morality," not, it is important to note, because luxury and license are sinful and lead to damnation and hell but because the excessive gratification of physical desires, be they for sex or for alcohol, and any over-indulgence of one's selfish mental weaknesses reduce the energy and attention which the individual can offer to the state and to society.

The Bolsheviks do not believe in evolution in the realm of politics; they are revolutionists. Eighteenth and nineteenth-century liberalism tended toward the survival of the fittest. But the essence of the Russian revolution is the protection of the under dog, of the proletarian and peasant who, unaided, would not survive in the unequal struggle with the capitalist and land-owner. The function of the Soviet state is to support the oppressed majority against the vested and acquired interests of the economically powerful minority.

The doctrine of the survival of the fittest, translated into every-day life, permits freedom of action, as little restraint as possible, the freest play for nature and human nature. Communist doctrine involves the negation of individual freedom; human nature is discounted in the socialist scale of weights and measures; laissez-faire is replaced by discipline, if need be, by force. Only once did the Communists reveal a liberal vein. It was in their treatment of conscientious objectors during the civil wars. Russia has many sects such as the Dukhobors who are opposed to violence on grounds of conscience. Though the Government was engaged in a death struggle, it respected these sentiments. But in all else, whenever its own interests have been at stake, the state has disregarded the wishes and inclinations of the human unit. Liberty of the individual is not as sacred an ikon as it is in the West. To give economic freedom to the mass is a nobler aim. Thus the Communists would explain and justify (but in my opinion this does not justify) the absence of a free press in Russia and the activities of the G. P. U.

The aim of the Bolsheviks was not merely to overthrow one government and to establish their own. This was a means toward creating a new society. To that extent the Bolsheviks are as presumptuous as most reformers. In 1917 they must have argued to themselves much to this effect: "We are a minority. The majority has not invited us to rule it. But we know better than the majority what is good for it." In the interest of the new society a powerful state was set up. The powerful state was privileged to ride roughshod over the individual. The Bolsheviks presume to tell the individual how to act and how to live. This is the "superiority complex" which is one of the most essential characteristics of puritanism. "I am perfect. Watch me. Go thou and do likewise." The Russian Communists are puritans without religion.

In matters of morals the Communists advocate and agitate but do not use force. Only in the case of members of the Communist Party do they interfere if the individual's actions are likely "directly or indirectly to discredit the party." (Such a phrase permits of the widest interpretation and misinterpretation.) Thus in an article in the *Pravda* on The Party and Personal Life, O. Zortzeva, an official of the Central Control Committee, writes that "not long ago one of the representatives of the Control Committee in the South asked for instructions to combat the evil of divorce." She cites an instance (and there must be many more such instances) where a Communist was required to explain why he left his wife. He replied he could not live with her because she was unfit to mingle in the society of his new friends and acquaintances. The reply was regarded as unsatisfactory. The Soviet state enforces a most liberal divorce law. But the Communists discourage divorce. Within the party it is looked upon with disfavor.

The war, the revolution, the civil wars have worked havoc with the Russian family. It is perhaps no exaggeration to say that family life is crumbling. Trotzky, who has given more active attention to these questions of personal behavior than any other Communist leader, seeks to reënforce the collapsing buttresses of the family. (It will be recalled that Engels, the author with Marx of the "Communist Manifesto," wrote the "Origin of the Family" to prove that the family was a new, unnecessary, and reactionary institution.) Trotzky urges the "communalization of the family household" so as to "disencumber the family of kitchen and laundry." Take the burden of washing, cooking, sewing, child-raising from the family and "the relation between husband and wife will be cleansed of all that is external, foreign, forced, accidental. Each would cease to spoil the life of the other. . . ."

The family life of most Communist leaders would probably find favor in the eyes of the Bishop of New York, and we can imagine that Cotton Mather, if he returned to the flesh and visited Moscow, would hurry to Trotzky, slap him untheologically on the back, and say, "Thou art a man." There was something ascetic and impersonal in the way Lenin used to live. There is something reminiscent of Christian self-abnegation in Chicherin's, Bukharin's, Radek's disdain for good clothes. A Communist is required to contribute to the party treasury all the

salary he earns above $95 a month. And even
if his writings bring him a supplementary income he must not spend it for luxuries. The
Communists are the shock troops of the Soviet
régime. They must be like athletes in training.
They must not consume mental and spiritual ice
creams and pastries.

Alexandra Kollontai, now Soviet ambassador
in Christiania, stands for the utmost freedom in
sexual relations. But a review in the official
press of her book, "Love Among Laboring
Bees," stigmatizes her views on the subject as
"prostitution" and "intellectual tomfoolery."
"It is imperative," reads the last sentence of the
criticism, "to guard against the harmful influence of Comrade Kollontai." This is the attitude which in other countries leads to the ap-
pointment of vice censors. Russia, fortunately,
is too advanced to subject itself to such a humili-
ation. Only the lives of Communists are cen-
sored. In respect to the great mass of the people
the Bolsheviks content themselves with preach-
ing.

Trotzky's sermons will certainly do the people no harm. Russians have barely a trace of

puritanism. Take the instance of their famous, many-ply "mother" oaths. Beside them the worst product of the British navvy looks pale. Says Trotzky: "One would have to consult philologists, linguists, and folk-lore experts to find out whether any other people has such unrestrained, filthy, and disgusting oaths as we have. As far as I know, there is no other." The Communists have initiated an anti-swearing campaign. In some factories the workers themselves decided to fine any one who used an "expression." Wherever one goes, in industrial plants, in beer saloons, in clubs, one sees the colored "Don't Swear" poster. Even in the army, where curses once found their most fertile field, they are becoming increasingly rare.

A Communist should not play cards. A member of the party will not, if he is a good Communist, enter a gambling casino. (The Moscow gambling casinos, incidentally, have been closed by order of the Government.) Newly initiated Communists ask their instructors whether they are to permit their wives to powder their faces. A Communist would hardly come to her office with her lips rouged and even non-Communist workers in many Soviet commissariats feel that it is bad form to use the lipstick. Certainly very few if any women Communists dress to fashion. Most of them dress badly. There are more serious things to do than to mind the clothes on one's back. It is unworthy of a Communist, and Communists think it is unworthy of all Russians, to give too much thought to the flesh. I know a non-Communist Soviet official who likes to carry a cane, but he leaves it home when he goes to work.

There can be no let-up, says Trotzky, in the war against alcohol. The Government has abolished vodka, but the bootleg "samogonka" has replaced it. The police arrest men and women (in Russia most of the apprehended bootleggers are women) but force removes as little of the evil here as it does in the United States. So strong is the drink tradition in Russia that even many Communists indulge in the permissible wines and light beers. But the party reminds its members that they must inhibit such desires. It will not do for the best soldiers of the state and the master-builders of a new society to be-

come inebriated, or lose their heads and time in
the pursuit of women, or play cards, or stop to
adjust their neckties while the foundations of
the structure are being laid.

Stereotypes
By Florence Guy Seabury

Florence Guy Seabury

is a frequent contributor to the New Republic *and
to various popular magazines.*

STEREOTYPES

BY FLORENCE GUY SEABURY

IF Clarissa Harlow could have stepped out of her pre-Victorian world to witness some of the women stevedores and "longshoremen" now at work along the New York water front, she would certainly have fainted so abruptly that no masculine aid could have restored consciousness. If we can believe the 1920 census, a goodly number of Clarissa's timid and delicate sex are toiling gloriously in the most dangerous and violent occupations. Nor are they only engaged in handling steel beams and freight, running trucks and donkey engines, but as miners and steeplejacks, aviators and divers, sheriffs and explorers —everything, in fact that man ever did or thought of doing. They have proved, moreover, as successful in such a new occupation as capturing jungle tigers as in the old one of hunting husbands, as deft in managing big business as in running a little household.

But the census bureau, compiling all the facts of feminine industry, forgot to note that woman might perform these amazingly varied operations, outside the home, without changing in any measurable degree the rooted conception of her nature and activities. She may step out of skirts into knickers, cut her hair in a dozen short shapes and even beat a man in a prize fight, but old ideas as to her place and qualities endure. She changes nothing as set as the stereotyped image of her sex which has persisted since Eve.

The Inquiring Reporter of the New York *Sun* recently asked five persons whether they would prefer to be tried by a jury of men or women. "Of men," cried they all—two women and three men. "Women would be too likely to overlook the technical points of the law." "Women are too sentimental." "They are too easily swayed by an eloquent address." "Women are by nature sentimental." Almost anybody could complete the list. Ancient opinions of women's characteristics have been so widely advertised that the youngest child in the kindergarten can chirp the whole story. Billy, aged ten, hopes fervently that this country may never have a woman president. "Women haven't the brains—it's a man's job." A. S. M. Hutchinson, considerably older than Billy, has equally juvenile fears: that the new freedom for women may endanger her functions in the home. Whatever and wherever the debate, the status and attributes of women are settled by neat and handy generalizations, passed down from father to son, and mother to daughter. For so far, most women accept the patterns made for them and are as likely as not to consider themselves the weaker vessel, the more emotional sex, a lay figure of biological functioning.

Optimists are heralding a changed state in the relationship of men and women. They point to modern activities and interests as evidence of a different position in the world. They say that customs and traditions of past days are yielding to something freer and finer. The old order, as far as home life is concerned, has been turned topsy-turvy. Out of this chaos, interpreters of the coming morality declare that already better and happier ways have been established between man and maid.

It sounds plausible enough, but the trouble remains, that, so far, it isn't true. The intimate relationship of men and women is about as it was in the days of Cleopatra or Xanthippe. The most brawny stevedorette leaves her freight in the air when the whistle blows and rushes home to husband as if she were his most sheltered possession. Following the tradition of the centuries, the business woman, whose salary may double that of her mate, hands him her pay envelope and asks permission to buy a new hat. Busts and bustles are out, flat chests and orthopedic shoes are in, while the waist line moves steadily toward the thigh— but what of it? Actualities of present days leave the ancient phantasies unchanged.

Current patterns for women, as formulated by the man in the street, by the movies, in the women's clubs and lecture halls can be boiled down to one general cut. Whatever she actually is or does, in the stereotype she is a creature specialized to function. The girl on the magazine cover is her symbol. She holds a mirror, a fan, a flower and—at Christmas—a baby. Without variety, activity, or individuality her sugary smile pictures satisfying femininity. Men are allowed diversity. Some are libertines, others are husbands; a few are lawyers, many are clerks.

They wear no insignia of masculinity or badge of paternity and they are never expected to live up to being Man or Mankind. But every woman has the whole weight of formulated Womanhood upon her shoulders. Even in new times, she must carry forward the design of the ages.

One of the quaint hang-overs of the past is that men are the chief interpreters of even the modern woman. It may be that the conquest of varied fields and the strain of establishing the right to individuality has taken all her time and energy. Or it may be that the habit of vicarious expression has left her inarticulate. Whatever it is, in the voluminous literature of the changing order, from the earnest tracts on "How It Feels to Be a Woman," by a leading male educator to the tawdry and flippant syndicated views of W. L. George, masculine understanders take the lead. And the strange part of their interpretations is that they run true to ancient form. Old adages are put in a more racy vernacular, the X-ray is turned on with less delicacy, but when the froth of their engaging frankness disappears, hoary old ideas remain thickly in the tumbler.

Take the intimate life story of a girl of the

younger generation—Janet March—written by
that good friend of women, Floyd Dell. The
blurb on the jacket of the book announces that
she moves toward "not a happy ending but an intelligent one." And the end? Janet finds her
mate and the curtain falls to the soft music of
maternity. "One has to risk something," Janet
cries. "All my life I've wanted to *do* something
with myself. Something exciting. And this is
the one thing I can do. I can"—she hesitated.
"I can create a breed of fierce and athletic girls,
new artists, musicians, and singers."

As a conclusion this is acceptable to any one
with a heart, but wherein is it intellectual and
not happy? Queen Victoria, the Honorable
Herbert Asquith, or the Reverend Lyman Abbott would be equally pleased by its one hundred
per cent womanliness. And how does it differ
from our cherished slogan, "Woman's place is in
the home"? Only because Floyd Dell cuts Janet
in a large, free-hand design. The advance pattern calls for a wealth of biological and gyne-
cological explanation, pictures the girl as a
healthy young animal who "smoked but drew
the line on grounds of health at inhaling," and,

following the fashion of peasants in foreign countries, consummated the marriage before it was celebrated. Yet Janet, who claimed her right to all experience and experiment, finally raises her banner on the platform of fireside and nursery.

Despite its unquestionable orthodoxy, Janet March was retired from circulation. But no one has successfully dammed the flowing tide of W. L. George. He draws with somewhat futuristic effect, at times, but his conclusions are those of the old masters. "No woman," he enunciates authoritatively, "values her freedom until she is married and then she is proud to surrender it to the man she has won." Or take this: "All women are courtesans at heart, living only to please the other sex." Wherein does this differ from the sentiment of Alexander Pope who, one hundred and fifty or more years before the birth of W. L. George, declared:

> Men, some to business, some to pleasures take,
> But every woman is at heart a rake.

H. L. Mencken, stirred by debates about the intelligence of woman and her newer activities, essayed "In Defense of Women," to put his old

wine in a fancy bottle, but it was the same home
brew. Generously conceding brains to women,
he proves his point on the evidence that they are
used to ensnare men, who weak-minded and
feeble in flight are usually bowled over in the
battle of wits. "Marriage," he says, "is the best
career a woman can reasonably aspire to—and
in the case of very many women, the only one
that actually offers a livelihood." . . . "A child-
less woman remains more than a little ridiculous
and ill at ease." . . . "No sane woman has ever
actually muffed a chance." . . . "The majority
of inflammatory suffragettes of the sex hygiene
and birth control species are simply those who
have done their best to snare a man and failed."

In H. L. Mencken's favor is his absence of the
usual gush about feminine beauty. He declares
with refreshing honesty that in contrast to the
female body a milk jug or even a cuspidor is a
thing of intelligent and gratifying design. Of
woman's superior mental ability he says, "A cave
man is all muscle and mush. Without a woman
to think for him, he is truly a lamentable spectacle, a baby with whiskers, a rabbit with the
frame of an aurochs, a feeble and preposterous

caricature of God." What a pity that women use all these advantages of superior mentality and ability only in the age-old game of man-hunting. But do they?

D. H. Lawrence shares this philosophy of the chief business of women, and he is much more gloomy about it. In fact, he is decidedly neurotic in his fear of the ultimate absorption of man. Woman he describes perpetually as a great, magnetic womb, fecund, powerful, drawing, engulfing. Man he sees as a pitiful, struggling creature, ultimately devoured by fierce maternal force. "You absorb, absorb," cries Paul to Miriam in "Sons and Lovers," "as if you must fill yourself up with love because you've got a shortage somewhere." The Lawrence model, madly, fiercely possessive, differs from older forms in the abundance of physiological and pathological trimming. His conclusion, as voiced again by Paul to Miriam is, "A woman only works with part of herself; the real and vital part is covered up." And this hidden reality is her terrific, destructive, fervid determination to drown man in her embrace.

So it goes. To Floyd Dell woman is a Mother,

to H. L. Mencken a Wife, to W. L. George a
Courtesan, and to D. H. Lawrence a Matrix—
always specialized to sex. There may be men
who are able to think of woman apart from the
pattern of function, but they are inarticulate.
Most of them spend their lives associating with
a symbol. The set pieces they call Mary, Mar-
tha, Elaine, or Marguerite may follow the standardized design of grandmother, mother, or aunt.
Or in more advanced circles, the pattern may call
for bobbed hair, knickers, and cigarette case.
Under any form of radicalism or conservatism
the stereotype remains.

The old morality was built upon this body of
folk-lore about women. Whether pictured as a
chaste and beautiful angel, remote and untainted
by life's realities, or more cynically regarded as
a devil and the source of sin, the notion was always according to pattern. Naturally, the relationship of men and women has been built upon
the design, and a great many of our social ideals
and customs follow it. The angel concept led,
of course, to the so-called double standard which
provides for a class of Victorian dolls who per-
sonify goodness, while their sisters, the prosti-

tutes, serve as sacrificial offerings to the wicked
ways of men. The new morality, as yet rather
nebulous and somewhat mythical, has fewer class
distinctions. The angel picture, for instance, has
had some rude blows. As portrayed by the van-
guard of radicals and interpreters, however, the
changing conventions have their roots in the old
generalizations and phantasies.

Perhaps this is only to be expected, for the man
or woman does not exist whose mind has not become so filled with accepted ideas of human beings and relationships before maturity, or even
adolescence, that what is seen thereafter is
chiefly a fog of creeds and patterns. If several
hundred babies, children of good inherited back-
grounds, could be brought up on an isolated
island, without a taint of superimposed custom
and never hearing generalizations about themselves—never having standardized characteristics laid heavily upon their shoulders, perhaps a
different type of relationship founded upon actualities, would be evolved. Without a mythology
of attributes, based chiefly upon biological functions, real human beings might discover each
other and create new and honest ways of com-

radeship and association. As it is to-day, we do not know what the pristine reactions of individuals, free from the modifications of stereotype, would be like.

It was the development of means by which beliefs could be separated from actual facts which brought modern science into being and freed the world from the quaint superstitions of the ages. Not until the nature of substance could be proved and classified in contrast with the mass of ignorant notions which clogged ancient thought was the amazing mechanical, economic, and scientific advance of the last century possible. The world of antiquity had standardized life and tied thought down to speculative creeds. Empirical science discarded all supposition and centered itself upon building up another picture—life as an examination of its actual nature proved it to be.

In the creating of a new order which will bring with it a different type of social and personal contact, something similar must take place. For most of our ideas, even those classified as liberal and advanced, are built upon the reactions of an alleged, not an actual human being.

Men have suffered from pattern-making, but never have they been burdened with the mass of generalizations that are heaped upon women from birth. Nobody knows what women are really like because our minds are so filled with the stereotype of Woman. And this picture, even in the interpretations of those who claim to understand the modern woman, is chiefly of function, not character. It is impossible to create a satisfying relationship between a red-blooded individual and a symbol. A changed morality cannot successfully emerge when half of those who participate are regarded not as people but functions. As long as women are pictured chiefly as wife, mother, courtesan—or what not —defining merely a relationship to men—nothing new or strange or interesting is likely to happen. The old order is safe.

Women and the New Morality
By Beatrice M. Hinkle

Beatrice M. Hinkle

is a physician and psycho-analyst who follows in general the beliefs of Jung. She is the author of "Recreating the Individual."

WOMEN AND THE NEW MORALITY

BY BEATRICE M. HINKLE, M.D.

IN the general discussions of morality which are the fashion just now, sex morality seems to occupy the chief place. Indeed, judging from the amount of talk on this subject one would be inclined to think it the outstanding problem of our time. Certainly the whole of humanity is concerned in and vitally affected by the sexual aspect of life. Sexuality in its capacity as an agent of transformation is the source of power underlying the creativeness of man. In its direct expression, including its influence upon human relationships in general, it is woman's particular concern. The position of importance it is assuming seems, therefore, to be justified, regardless of the protests of the intellect and the wish of the ego to minimize its significance.

A general weakening of traditional standards of ethics and morals and their gradual loss of control over the conduct of individuals have long

been observed in other activities—in business affairs and in the world of men's relations with
each other. This has taken place so quietly and
with so much specious rationalizing that sharp
practices and shady conduct which formerly
would have produced scandals, shame, and social taboos now scarcely cause a protest from
society. These aspects of morality belong to the
masculine world in particular and produce little
agitation, while the upheaval in sex morals particularly affects the feminine world and by many
people can scarcely be considered calmly enough
for an examination. The changes in this field
are the most recent and are being produced by
women; they are taking place in full view of all
with no apologies and with little hesitation.
They appear, therefore, most striking and dis-
turbing. It can be said that in the general dis-
integration of old standards, women are the active agents in the field of sexual morality and
men the passive, almost bewildered accessories
to the overthrow of their long and firmly organ-
ized control of women's sexual conduct.

The old sex morality, with its double standard,
has for years been criticized and attacked by

fair-minded persons of both sexes. It has been recognized that this unequal condition produced effects as unfortunate for the favored sex as for the restricted one, and that because of this it could not be maintained indefinitely by a psychologically developing people. As a matter of course, whenever the single standard was mentioned, the standard governing women was invariably meant, and the fact was ignored that it is easier to break down restrictions than to force them upon those who have hitherto enjoyed comparative freedom. Furthermore, it was not realized that a sex morality imposed by repression and the power of custom creates artificial conceptions and will eventually break down.

This forced morality is in fact at the present time quite obviously disintegrating. We see women assuming the right to act as their impulses dictate with much the same freedom that men have enjoyed for so long. The single standard is rapidly becoming a *fait accompli,* but instead of the standard identified with women it is nearer the standard associated with men. According to a universal psychological law, actual reality eventually overtakes and replaces the cultural ideal.

Although this overthrow of old customs and sex ideals must be chiefly attributed to the economic independence of women brought about through the industrialism of our age, it is safe to say that no man thought ahead far enough or understood the psychology of women sufficiently to anticipate the fruit of this economic emancipation. As long as women were dependent upon men for the support of themselves and their children there could be no development of a real morality, for the love and feelings of the woman were so intermingled with her economic necessities that the higher love impulse was largely undifferentiated from the impulse of self-preservation. True morality can only develop when the object or situation is considered for itself, not when it is bound up with ulterior and extraneous elements which vitiate the whole. The old morality has failed and is disintegrating fast, because it was imposed from without instead of evolving from within.

A morality which has value for all time and is not dependent upon custom or external cultural fashions can arise only from a high development of the psychological functions of thinking and feeling, with the developed individual as the determiner of values instead of general custom or some one else's opinion. The function of feeling and the realm of the emotions have been universally regarded as woman's special province; therefore it is women who are specially concerned with testing out moral values involving sexual behavior. Women have been reproached by men again and again as being only sexual creatures, and they have meekly accepted the reproach. Now, instead of examining the statement, they have accepted the sexual problem of men as though it were their own, and with it the weight of man's conflict and his articulateness. For sexuality as a problem and a conflict definitely belongs to man's psychology; it is he primarily who has been ashamed of his domination by this power and has struggled valiantly to free himself; his egotistic and sexual impulses have always been at war with each other. But whoever heard of women being ashamed of yielding to the power of love? Instead they gloried in the surrender of themselves and counted themselves blessed when love ruled. It is this need of man to escape from the power of the sensual appeal that has made him scorn sex and look upon the great creative power of life as something shameful and inferior, and in modern days treat it as a joke or with the indifferent superficiality which betrays emasculation and inadequacy.

One has only to "listen in" where any large group of men, young or old, are gathered together in easy familiarity (the army camps were recent examples on a large scale) to discover the degree to which sexuality still dominates the minds of men, even though its expression is confined so largely to the jocose and the obscene. Many men can corroborate this report from a military camp—"we have sexuality in all its dirty and infantile forms served daily for breakfast, lunch, and dinner." It is the inferior and inadequate aspect of masculine sexuality that has made it necessary for man to conceive it as something shameful and unclean, and to insist that woman must carry his purity for him and live the restrictions and suppression that rightly belonged to him. Woman on her part became an easy victim of his ideas and convictions, because of the very fact that the function of feeling and the emotions so largely dominate her psychology. The translation of feeling into thought-forms has been slow and difficult. About herself woman has been quite inarticulate and largely unconscious. This inarticulateness inevitably made her accept man's standards and values for her, for little directed thinking is achieved without form and words. Because of her sexual fertility and fruitfulness woman had no sexual conflict; therefore, man easily unloaded his psychological burden upon her, and claimed freedom for the satisfaction of his own desires.

Thus, woman was made a symbol or personification of man's morality. She had to live for him that which he was unable to live for himself. This was the reason for his indignation at moral transgressions on her part. She had injured the symbol and revealed his weakness to him. However, with the discovery by women that they could be economically independent of men, they commenced to find themselves interesting. As they have gradually come to think for themselves about fundamental questions, there has begun a tremendous activity and busyness in regard to the very subject which was previously taboo.

A recent writer boasts that men have changed their attitude regarding sexual problems very little and are not much concerned in the new interest of women. This is probably true, for man has contributed all he has to give to the subject. He has laid down his taboos and externalized his restrictions, chiefly applicable to the other sex, and he is finished with the subject—bored by having it thrust forward as an unfinished problem needing reconsideration. All of his knowledge or understanding of the sexual aspect of life—the aspect underlying human creativeness, the faulty development of which is responsible for a large part of his woes, "can be told in two hours to any intelligent sixteen year old boy," another writer recently stated. It is this youthful ignorance and assurance that the last word has been spoken on this subject that has awakened women, no longer dependent economically, to the fact that they must also become independent of men intellectually if they wish to gain expression for their knowledge or to form their own rules of conduct based on their psychology. In the true scientific spirit of the age they are now experimenting and using nature's method of trial and error to find out for themselves by conscious living experience what feeling has vaguely told them. This is the first step towards objectifying and clarifying woman's intuitive knowledge.

With the revolt of women against the old restrictions and the demand for freedom to experience for themselves, there has appeared a most significant phase of the changed morality —the new relation of women toward each other. The significance of this enormous change which has been taking place very quietly and yet very rapidly is scarcely appreciated. However, when one realizes that only a generation ago the newspapers were still publishing their funny paragraphs at the expense of women ("The dear creatures; how they love one another"), the great difference in their relations today becomes evident. The generally accepted distinction between the personal loyalties of the sexes can be summed up in the statement that women are loyal in love and disloyal in friendship, while men are loyal in friendship and disloyal in love. It is this attitude of women that is gradually disappearing with the awakening of a new sense of themselves as individuals. Their changed attitude towards each other—the recognition of their own values, and the growing realization that only in solidarity can any permanent impression be made on the old conception of woman as an inferior, dependent creature, useful for one purpose only—constitutes the most marked difference between their present social condition and that of the past.

As long as women remained psychologically unawakened, their individual values were swallowed up in their biological value for the race. They were under the unconscious domination of their sexual fruitfulness and an enemy of themselves as individuals. Weininger gives as the chief difference between the masculine and feminine creeds that "Man's religion consists in a supreme belief in himself—woman's in a supreme belief in other people." These other people being men, the sex rivalry among women that has so long stood in the way of their further development is easily understood. It has been a vicious circle which could only be broken by women's gaining another significance in the eyes of the world and in their own eyes. This other significance is the economic importance which they have acquired in the world of men.

It makes little difference within the social structure how many individual women exist who have forged a position for themselves and have won a freedom and independence equal to that possessed by the ordinary man, so long as they are isolated phenomena having little understanding of the peculiar difficulties and problems of women as a whole, and no relation with each other. These women have always existed in all culture periods, but they have produced little effect upon the social condition or psychology of women in general. There was no group action because the majority of women were inarticulate. The woman who was different became abnormal in the eyes of the world.

This lack of an adequate self-consciousness among women, their general inability to translate feeling into form capable of being understood by the masculine mind, accounts for their acceptance of the statements made about them by men in an effort to understand creatures apparently so different from themselves. There is no doubt that woman's inarticulateness about herself, even when her feelings were very different from those she was told were normal, has been responsible for a vast amount of the nonsense written about her.

This passive acceptance of the opinions of others has been most disastrous for woman's development. Her superior psychological processes consist of feelings and intuitions, and when these are stultified or violated by being forced into a false relation, or are inhibited from development, the entire personality is crippled. The inadequate development of the function of thought and the dominating rôle played by the function of feeling in the psychology of woman have produced an obviously one-sided effect and have caused men to postulate theories about her, which are given forth as though they were the last word to be said—fixed and unchangeable. Indeed the statement that women are incapable of change and that no growth is possible for them is one of the favorite assertions of the masculine writers upon the subject of women's psychology. As the present is the first time in our historical period in which there has been any general opportunity for women as a whole to think for themselves and to develop in new ways, the basis for this assertion does not exist, and it obviously conceals an unconscious wish that women should not change.

The effect of collective ideas and cultural traditions upon the personality is immeasurable. The greatest general change that is taking place today is the weakening of these ideas and the refusal of women to be bound by them. Women are for the first time demanding to live the forbidden experiences directly and draw conclusions on this basis. I do not mean to imply that traditional moral standards controlling woman's sexual conduct have never been transgressed in the past. They have very frequently been transgressed, but secretly and without inner justification. The great difference today lies in the open defiance of these customs with feelings of entire justification, or even a non-recognition of a necessity for justification. In other words, there has arisen a feeling of moral rightness in the present conduct, and wrongness in the former morality. Actually the condition is one in which natural, long-restrained desire is being substituted for collective moral rules, and individuals are largely becoming a law unto themselves. It is difficult to predict what will be the result of the revolt, but it is certain that this is the preceding condition which renders it possible for a new morality in the real sense to be born within the individual. It has already produced the first condition of all conscious psychic development —a moral conflict—and woman has gained a problem.

In the general chaos of conflicting feelings she is losing her instinctive adaptation to her biological rôle as race bearer, and is attempting adaptation to man's reality. She is making the effort to win for herself some differentiation and development of the ego function apart from her instinctive processes. This is the great problem confronting woman today; how can she gain a relation to both racial and individual obligations, instead of possessing one to the exclusion of the other? Must she lose that which has been and still is her greatest strength and value? I for one do not think so, although I am fully conscious of the tremendous psychic effort and responsibility involved in the changing standards. It is necessary that women learn to accept themselves and to value themselves as beings possessing a worth at least equal to that of the other sex, instead of unthinkingly accepting standards based on masculine psychology. Then women will recognize the necessity of developing their total psychic capacities just as it is necessary for men to do, but they will see that this does not involve imitation of men or repudiation of their most valuable psychic functioning. The real truth is that it has at last become apparent to many women that men cannot redeem them.

It is not the purpose of this article to deal with the practical issues involved in the new moral freedom. One thing however is clearly evident: Women are demanding a reality in their relations with men that heretofore has been lacking, and they refuse longer to cater to the traditional notions of them created by men, in which their true feelings and personalities were disregarded and denied. This is the first result of the new morality.

Family in America

AN ARNO PRESS / NEW YORK TIMES COLLECTION

Abbott, John S. C. **The Mother at Home:** Or, The Principles of Maternal Duty. 1834.

Abrams, Ray H., editor. **The American Family in World War II.** 1943.

Addams, Jane. **A New Conscience and an Ancient Evil.** 1912.

The Aged and the Depression: Two Reports, 1931–1937. 1972.

Alcott, William A. **The Young Husband.** 1839.

Alcott, William A. **The Young Wife.** 1837.

American Sociological Society. **The Family.** 1909.

Anderson, John E. **The Young Child in the Home.** 1936.

Baldwin, Bird T., Eva Abigail Fillmore and Lora Hadley. **Farm Children.** 1930.

Beebe, Gilbert Wheeler. **Contraception and Fertility in the Southern Appalachians.** 1942.

Birth Control and Morality in Nineteenth Century America: Two Discussions, 1859–1878. 1972.

Brandt, Lilian. **Five Hundred and Seventy-Four Deserters and Their Families.** 1905. Baldwin, William H. **Family Desertion and Non-Support Laws.** 1904.

Breckinridge, Sophonisba P. **The Family and the State:** Select Documents. 1934.

Calverton, V. F. **The Bankruptcy of Marriage.** 1928.

Carlier, Auguste. **Marriage in the United States.** 1867.

Child, [Lydia]. **The Mother's Book.** 1831.

Child Care in Rural America: Collected Pamphlets, 1917–1921. 1972.

Child Rearing Literature of Twentieth Century America, 1914–1963. 1972.

The Colonial American Family: Collected Essays, 1788–1803. 1972.

Commander, Lydia Kingsmill. **The American Idea.** 1907.

Davis, Katharine Bement. **Factors in the Sex Life of Twenty-Two Hundred Women.** 1929.

Dennis, Wayne. **The Hopi Child.** 1940.

Epstein, Abraham. **Facing Old Age.** 1922. New Introduction by Wilbur J. Cohen.

The Family and Social Service in the 1920s: Two Documents, 1921–1928. 1972.

Hagood, Margaret Jarman. **Mothers of the South.** 1939.

Hall, G. Stanley. **Senescence:** The Last Half of Life. 1922.

Hall, G. Stanley. **Youth:** Its Education, Regimen, and Hygiene. 1904.

Hathway, Marion. **The Migratory Worker and Family Life.** 1934.

Homan, Walter Joseph. **Children & Quakerism.** 1939.

Key, Ellen. **The Century of the Child.** 1909.

Kirchwey, Freda. **Our Changing Morality:** A Symposium. 1930.

Kopp, Marie E. **Birth Control in Practice.** 1934.

Lawton, George. **New Goals for Old Age.** 1943.

Lichtenberger, J. P. **Divorce:** A Social Interpretation. 1931.

Lindsey, Ben B. and Wainwright Evans. **The Companionate Marriage.** 1927. New Introduction by Charles Larsen.

Lou, Herbert H. **Juvenile Courts in the United States.** 1927.

Monroe, Day. **Chicago Families.** 1932.

Mowrer, Ernest R. **Family Disorganization.** 1927.

Reed, Ruth. **The Illegitimate Family in New York City.** 1934.

Robinson, Caroline Hadley. **Seventy Birth Control Clinics.** 1930.

Watson, John B. **Psychological Care of Infant and Child.** 1928.

White House Conference on Child Health and Protection. **The Home and the Child.** 1931.

White House Conference on Child Health and Protection. **The Adolescent in the Family.** 1934.

Young, Donald, editor. **The Modern American Family.** 1932.